# Chronicles

COVERED & REVEALED

## Alisa J. Henley

KANSAS CITY, MO

Alisa Henley, PO Box 683, Grandview, MO 64030 - www.u-shine.org

Scripture Quotations and References taken from:

Cover Drawing: Lee Collins
Interior Design: The Sunshine Organization

Chronicles, Covered & Revealed by Alisa Henley. —1st ed.
ISBN-13: 978-0692275184
ISBN-10: 0692275185

## *Thanks and Acknowledgements*

- Thank you to my mother, Jane Henley, and my entire family for always supporting my God-ordained endeavors.

- Jennifer C. Hogan, you are the best for proofreading all of my books.

- Lee Collins, one of the greatest artists I know. Thank you for providing the artwork for the cover.

- I especially thank all Christian singles who provided content.

- Thank you to my Church family–Spruce St. Matthew, you rock!

Dedicated to every Christian single committed to living a victorious life in Christ. Singleness is the perfect opportunity to pursue Christ with a whole heart!

# Contents

"I had struggled so hard and so long that I had simply exhausted myself, only to find that God had all the time in the world to wait for me to allow Him to free me."

—Michelle McKinney Hammond

# Beautiful Heart . . .

Lyrics by Tricky: Wait For God

*I wait for God, and it's hard*

*I am the Lamb, I don't understand*

*I drink your Blood, and I'm still thirsty*

*I wait for God, and it's hard*

The lyrics to this song remind me of every Christian single I have met over the years. No question that singleness is God's joy, but there are times when it's not the single's joy. Logically, the longer the journey the easier it should get. Instead, I have had to learn ways of coping and riding the waves of being single. Fifteen years down the line, the challenges of being single still carry the same intensity level. Reaching a higher level of maturity on this journey creates destiny and potential to live a meaningful single life. This does not mean that challenges will not arise or temptation will not come; but you and I can be purpose-driven singles. You and I are single for a reason: to build our testimony and usher us into wholeness. In Philippians 1:20, Paul says he cannot wait to continue on his course no matter his state of living; he strives to make Christ more known. Paul wrote and organized this appeal to build rapport, persuade the mind, and move the emotions. Like Paul, God's grace is enough for your outcome.

To every Christian single: God has a plan for you and it is perfect. Since before time began, God has had each of us in mind (heart) for essential roles in the divine plan. We are not just cogs in a giant wheel. We are chosen, called, and sent forth in the name of the Lord Jesus Christ. It is the last part that is most challenging. We find it difficult to believe that God gives us everything we need when we ask for it. God's plan takes trust and doesn't always offer the luxury of knowing what is next. You and I must remember that if we say YES to God, He will give us all that we need to be the best husband, wife, mother, father, religious single person, priest—whatever it is to which He calls us.

This journey of singleness has taught me to surrender my whole heart to Christ—sometimes broken along the way—but there was always healing and restoration in the heartbreak. Loving God will not end the challenges of sexual temptation, loneliness, pressure, or discontentment. "For no temptation (no trial regarded as enticing to sin), [no matter how it comes or where it leads] has overtaken you and laid hold on you that is not common to man [that is, no temptation or trial has come to you that is beyond human resistance and that is not adjusted and adapted and belonging to human experience, and such as man can bear]. But God is faithful [to His Word and to His compassionate nature], and He [can be trusted] not to let you be tempted and tried and assayed beyond your ability and strength of resistance and power to endure, but with the temptation He will [always] also provide the way out (the means of escape to a landing place), that you may be capable and strong and powerful to bear up under it patiently" (1 Cor. 10:13, AMP).

This book is not a guide to finding your mate. It was written to teach you how to live a victorious life, overcome pressures and challenges, and walk in wholeness. Not giving in to pressure and experiencing peace lends your soul to waiting on God and placing your expectation in Him. Life happens for a reason and season. You can't define the terms of life's events. We wish to live our lives as if we can skip from 1st grade to 12th grade, as if none of the training gained in grades 2 through 11 is necessary. We go through phases, or various states of being, for a reason. God uses them to grow and develop us. Although it is true that most singles want to be married, very few prepare to be a husband or wife. Wisdom is the principle thing when preparing for God's call. I believe a major reason people rush into marriage is that they are tired of being single. They often are in love with the idea of being married—not the honor of marriage. Others are in such a hurry to be married that they will marry anyone who comes along, and then wonder why they are so miserable. You've tried everything else; now try waiting for God. Since most married people want to be single—and singles, married—finding the balance is difficult. I encourage you to live every day, from this day forward, with joy in your heart and viewing your season of singleness through God's lenses.

# CHAPTER 1

# Be You

To be a Christian single adult is a two-fold identity. You are seeking to follow Christ and you are not married. The Church considers you a single adult if you are over the age of 18 and if you have never been married or are divorced or widowed. When you are single, you do not have that one person upon whom you can rely. You have to turn to your family or friends when pressing issues emerge or emotions of any sort swell within you. It is ridiculous to believe life depends on being married or not. Many wonderful deserving people have yet to marry, and may not marry. Marriage is a step in this life journey. It has a different path, but that does not mean that you will not reach your final destination if you never have the opportunity to marry. Life for singles can assume a positive tilt when they:

- Live for God,
- Seek to know God,
- Seize opportunities to help others,
- Go places, rather than sit at home waiting to be discovered,
- Spend time on self-improvement, and
- Show faith that affirms their ability to make it in life.

Gordon B. Hinckley made a wonderful point about being single. Those who will not marry must face that fact, but continuous single status is not without opportunity, challenge, or generous recompense. Being Christian and single is not an easy path for many reasons. Collective mental and emotional scars, such as self-hate, fear of success, and jealousy play significant roles. Navigating life takes determination and hard work if one is to live by faith. Being Christian means choosing to be different from the rest of society. We live where wrong is often promoted as right, and where right is unpopular. Those who stand up and fight for right will risk being labeled as lame, oddball, or weird.

Difficulties arise from being a part of society. Single status brings vulnerability, weakened support systems, and few sources of consistent positive affirmation. However, despite these difficulties the single adult is the most eligible for successful living in this decade and beyond. God has called many to singleness for a part of their lives. Few understand the great honor it is to serve the Lord in this way. Marriage is blessed and ordained by God, but single life is also valuable: it allows people to commit their energy to serving Him. As seen throughout history, unmarried Christians have an incredible opportunity to influence this world with the Gospel. Singles make the mistake of putting their lives on hold until they marry. This idea is detrimental both to those singles and to the church. If every Christian recognized their value and used their talents to serve, they could meet all the needs of local churches. The entire world could be reached with the Gospel of Jesus Christ! Stop believing the "I am missing something" lie and accept the call to obey and serve God with your whole heart, mind, and strength. Marriage may or may not be God's plan for you. Live life now and trust God with your decisions. Single life could be better or worse than married life and comes with its own unique challenges. God may have you single for a variety of reasons, but the Bible in 1 Cor. 7:32-35, teaches:

- God can get your attention. When you are married, your focus is your spouse, not God.
- God is getting you ready to do a mighty work for Him. In-depth ministry work starts when you have to minister to the same person day in and day out.
- Spiritual matters matter. Your entire life is a spiritual matter with natural benefits and implications.

Some of you may be single by:

Circumstance
- No one has asked for your hand in marriage.
- You have not found the right spouse for you.
- You are divorced, widowed, or too young to marry.

Choice

- Perhaps you prefer to be single.
- You want to be like Paul.

Whether by circumstance or by choice, every Christian single can live covered or revealed. Advantages of singleness include freedom from care and freedom to serve the Lord—but with such freedom, danger is always lurking.

The most experienced danger is **PHYSICAL TEMPTATION OR INTIMACY**.

As a Christian, you are called to believe sex is reserved for marriage. God designed it that way to bring you into oneness with your spouse. You become one with whomever you share sexual intimacy. That's why you might stay in bad relationships—and when you break up it resembles divorce or tearing of the flesh. Physical temptation is every illegal sexual intercourse except that between a husband and wife. Pleasure with your hand or somebody else's hand; your mouth or somebody else's mouth; your sex toy or somebody else's—is illegal. The point is, "sex" is more than you penetrating someone or allowing someone to penetrate you; oral sex is sex. Enough Said! The message that sex before marriage is acceptable is everywhere. So the million-dollar question now becomes . . .

> MARRIAGE is **blessed** and **ordained** by God, but SINGLE life is also **valuable**: it allows people to **commit** their energy to serving Him.

Will God ignore this sin based on what society thinks? On the other hand, does He mean what He says?

In Matthew 15:9-20, God says that you defile your body when you give in to physical temptation. In short, you make yourself unclean, unholy, dirty, corrupt, and common. Keeping yourself is a heart issue. Defilement is caused by the sin's nature and sinful conduct. Any person who defiles the temple that God made a holy place is in opposition to God. Did you know that if a child of God sins against God, that child *chose* to commit an act of sin? Sin violates God's law and is contrary to how He wants you to live. Defilement of the temple shows the believer's accountability to a God of Judgment. Christians know how to act and behave because they have holy hearts. This is why the Bible says to "grieve not the Holy Spirit" and to "quench not the Spirit." Quench means to extinguish! To grieve is about your character and to quench has to do with the power of the Holy Spirit. There are no formulas or step-by-step processes to staying clean—just decisions and choices. Are you willing to forgo your physical desires to yield to the Holy Spirit?

> Do you not discern and understand that you [the whole church of Corinth] are God's temple (His Sanctuary), and that God's Spirit has His permanent dwelling in you [to be at home in you, collectively as a church and individually]? If anyone does hurt to God's temple or corrupts it [with false doctrines] or destroys it, God will do hurt to him and bring him to the corruption of death and destroy him. For the temple of God is holy (sacred to Him) and that [temple] you [the believing church and its individual believers] are. (1 Cor. 3:16-17, AMP)

Per Paul, no one will get away with vandalizing God's temple. In the movie Beat Street, a character found pleasure in spray-painting new, white commuter trains. When he would paint a train, another character would come behind him and vandalize his work. This went on until the culprit became comfortable in his actions. He eventually committed van-dalism while the other person was still there, creating the highest level of defiance. This act communicated that he did not care what the other per-son thought or how hard he worked. In addition, it did not matter that both were breaking the law. If you recall the movie, then you are well aware they scuffled and experienced their physical demise that day. If van-dalizing God's temple does not kill, it will hurt your witness and cause a hard-to-contain craving for physical intimacy.

Another danger is **LONELINESS**!

Many people perceive marriage as completion, thus perceiving single life as isolation. Marriage does not cure loneliness—millions of married people are lonely, too. No matter your stage in life, loneliness is unavoidable. Believing happiness is contingent on everything in life being perfect leads to a trap of postponing life-enriching experiences—like buying a house or taking a vacation—until you are married. Since we can't escape it, what can we do? Decide the role loneliness will play in our lives. Will loneliness dominate or will it submit? Are you relying on the wisdom of the Holy Spirit or on yourself when it comes to dealing with loneliness? You can choose to be a happy person with occasional times of loneliness, instead of a lonely person who experiences occasional happiness. Loneliness is a temptation, not a sin. Loneliness can be a temporary condition that departs in a few hours or days. Others times, it's a burden for weeks, months, or even years. Like a toothache, it's warning of a deeper problem and will grow worse if left unattended.

The first response to loneliness may be to self-medicate with busy work, retail therapy, or unwise choices about intimacy. Grocery shopping while hungry will cause you to buy items you normally pass up. The same thing happens when you "shop" for relationships while lonely. You become open to interactions that will rob you of focus. Loneliness indicates a relationship problem. There's more to overcoming loneliness than just surrounding yourself with people or using crowds instead of activities. The first four of the Ten Commandments speak to our relationship with God. The last six speak to our relationships with others. How is your relationship with God? Is it close and intimate, like that of a loving, caring parent and child? Or is your relationship with God distant and surface? Loneliness is God's way of drawing us closer to Him, then forcing us to reach out to other people. Improving relationships with others and letting them get close can be as unpleasant and dreaded as going to the dentist—but meaningful relationships take time and work.

From this day forward, denounce being a victim. A victim is attacked, injured, robbed, or killed by someone else; cheated or fooled by someone else; or harmed by an unpleasant event (such as an illness or accident). A victim accepts every adverse event as a personal attack instead of recognizing that misfortune befalls everyone. Playing the role of victim will always lead to bitterness. If you are suffering from loneliness, ask yourself if you have taken full possession of the abundant life God wants you to live. Are you spending regular quality time with your Heavenly Father? Are you active in a local church? Ask God to lead you into a deeper relationship with Him and greater involvement with fellow believers. Loneliness does not develop overnight it can result from a lifetime of influences that shape our personalities. Often, we are unaware of the subtle forces that can lead us into self-imposed isolation.

You have heard these suggestions from well-meaning friends: "Join an organization," or "You should develop a hobby." These are not unrealistic ideas, but neither are they solutions. Following are simple suggestions to break the chain of thoughts, emotions, and behaviors growing the root of loneliness. As always, pray for the wisdom of the Holy Spirit to guide you.

- Acknowledge the problem-You cannot overcome what you refuse to confront.
- Consider the causes-What triggers your loneliness?
- Accept what cannot be changed-God uses transitions to open doors to new experiences, but letting go of the old to receive the new is key.
- Make adjustments-Practice looking at yourself from God's perspective, and take part in community activities.
- Develop new habits-Organize your time and be sure to include outside activities. Make the most out of your time alone. Aloneness (as opposed to loneliness) can be a very positive experience. Aloneness gives you a chance to reflect on your life and to find healing for the wounds inflicted by the world. Many experts say we spend too little time alone. We are better off planning regular times of solitude in our lives.
- Make an effort to make new friends-Overcoming shyness and the fear of rejection are the biggest obstacles to initiating a friendship. Keep the following in mind as you try to prove new relationships:
  - Look for someone with whom you share a common interest.
  - Don't overwhelm a new acquaintance with your problems.
  - With time, the openness to express feelings will develop.
  - Give compliments and be thoughtful.
  - Refrain from giving unsolicited advice.
  - Be a good listener.

The last two dangers for singles are **PRESSURE AND CONTENTMENT**.

Many singles people get *pressure* from family, friends, society, and even their church. The expectation of marriage continues to rise the older you get. The Church focuses on couples and families, leaving singles longing to belong. I can't tell you how many times I've felt insignificant because I was unmarried. What others are saying about pressure...

Female, Age Range: 21-30

*I get pressure from my family to find a husband and father for my son. I was told by many to change my lifestyle to make myself more wholesome. We should change ourselves ONLY because we have put that object or security BEFORE our Creator and it has created a wall between Him and our salvation.*

Male, Age Range: 21-30

*Married friends? Try grandmothers in a hurry to have great-grandkids! I do have a number of married friends, but few if any of them pressure me on the issue. I remind them it's better to be single than to marry the wrong person, and they agree with me. Good things come to those who wait (upon the Lord).*

Female, Age Range: 31-40

*I'll never forget the day several relatives asked me if I was lesbian. The reason I don't view the whole relationship scene as the world does is that dating and one-night stands are not what God intended for us. I explained that my life, including my social life, is 100% in God's hands. My mother, a few years back, kept saying she wished I could be happy and be married. To this I replied, "Mom, I am happy. I don't know why you think otherwise. God blessed me with an incredible job, home, garden, an active lifestyle and ministry, and abundant friends around the world." Thereafter, I wrote her a letter explaining that through the years, her pressure for me to marry pushed us so far apart. I asked her to respect me as a grown adult peer and asked for her prayers.*

Male, Age Range: 31-40

*I get asked by friends, family, and church people, "When are you going to get married?" That used to be a difficult question. My answer: "When I believe the benefits of marriage outweigh that of single life." Now I treat it as a rhetorical question. Having a good mix of friends who aren't focused or concerned with that is what works best.*

Female, Age Range: 41-50

*I'm divorced for a great number of years now, but I feel pressured to get married from my own point of view. Most of my closest brothers and sisters in Christ are married. Of course, that is not a reason to get married. I have come to understand the significance of marriage in relation to the relationship we should have with our Lord and Savior Jesus Christ. I first need to Love the Lord with my heart, seek the Kingdom of God, and He will grant me the desires of my heart.*

Male, Age Range: 41-50

*How do I deal with friends who judge me for still being single? With a lot of patience and open-mindedness. Regarding people who are downright offensive in their attitude towards me (even though they aren't aware of it), talking with them is best.*

It can be difficult to overcome the pressure to marry and start a family. Married people with children pressure us to marry and have children as well. They are blessed in their relationships and want the same for us because they love us. Considering that people who pressure us mean well (even if they cause us pain or distress) makes it easier to take. We are not sinning because we haven't had the opportunity or inclination to marry and start a family.

The media and pop culture can feed discontentment in the soul of a Christian single. The quest to find purpose in a love relationship is found in song lyrics, movies, and reality TV. Our society is infused with the message that you are not "normal" and cannot be fulfilled unless you are attached to someone. In our materialistic information age, we are so prone to immediate gratification that it is difficult to accept what God allows. Paul said, "Not that I am implying that I was in any personal want, for I have learned how to be content (satisfied to the point where I am not disturbed or disquieted) in whatever state I am. I know how to be abased and live in straitened circumstances; and how to enjoy plenty and live in abundance. I have learned in any circumstance that secret of facing every situation, whether well fed or going hungry, having a sufficiency and enough to spare or going without and being in want. I have strength for all things in Christ who empowers me [I am ready for anything and equal to anything through Him who infuses inner strength into me; I am self-sufficient in Christ's sufficiency]" (Phil. 4:11-13, AMP).

On your journey of learning to be content, consider these jewels:

- Understand God's season of being single. True contentment in Christ means being satisfied with your relationship with the Almighty. It means cultivating a bond with God that will guide you when you do find someone who will see your value and be willing to accept your shortcomings. God's not saying you shouldn't be married. He's saying enrich your relationship with Him so you can love.

- Contentment flows from knowledge that God is in control and He arranges things IN HIS TIME. Ecclesiastes 3:1 teaches that everything under the sun has its season, and being anxious does not enhance one's love for either God or a potential spouse. We must understand that God's purpose for us is an abstract event in the future, but He gives us present-day assignments He wants us to be doing NOW!

- As Christians, we must accept the fact that not everyone is meant to marry. In Matthew 19:10-12, Jesus himself expounds that there are those who are born incapable of marriage, those who are made incapable by men, and those who made themselves incapable. God has admirable callings for those not married, too. The stigma we have placed on "singleness" is manmade; singleness has its place in God's Kingdom. Paul said in his first letter to the Corinthians, "But if they have not self-control (restraint of their passions), they should marry. For it is better to marry than to be aflame [with passions and tortured continually with ungratified desire]" (1 Cor. 7:9, AMP).

> True **CONTENTMENT** in Christ means being *satisfied* with your relationship with the **ALMIGHTY**.

Single life, whether temporary or long term, offers opportunities not available in married life. Single men and women, free from the responsibilities of pleasing a spouse, can focus their full attention on the Lord's work. More quiet time and privacy contribute to a deeper, richer spiritual life. More free hours during the week open the way for increased service to the extended family and the Church family. The Bible portrays notable singles who answered God's call to serve: Ruth, the young widow who devoted herself to providing for her mother-in-law, might be a faithful caregiver to someone in need. Anna, a long-time widow who spent day and night in the temple and greeted the infant Jesus could be a tireless worker within her congregation. Friends like Mary, Martha, and Lazarus who opened their home and hearts to Jesus during His ministry on earth are dependable friends. The apostle Paul might be the congregation's director of outreach or overseas mission. The four unmarried daughters of the evangelist Philip might be dynamic teachers. God makes no useless people. Indeed, singles have played and continue to play remarkable roles in His kingdom on earth. For this, He gives each of us unique talents, skills, and opportunities to serve Him—just as we are, where we are.

The basic recipe for oysters on the half shell can serve as the recipe for enjoying life as a Christian single. When you thought there was nothing more to learn from oysters, here's another lesson: You must clean the oyster and separate the meat from the shell before serving.

**Clean.** Clean up your perspective on life. You may feel as if you're lacking some-

thing because you are single. But if you are a Christian, you have received the most precious and most valuable gift in Jesus Christ. Although you may not have everything you want, you have much for which to be thankful. Be thankful for the gifts you've received, the blessings you now enjoy—and know that the best is yet to come! ". . . no good thing will He withhold from those who walk uprightly" (Ps. 84:11, NKJV).

**Separate.** Separate yourself from those things that are not pleasing to God. We

are *in* the world but not *of* the world, noting a difference in our lives. Our Christian single life should not mirror that of celebrities or non-Christian friends, because our primary goal is to do that which pleases God, not man. "Therefore come out from among them and be separate, says the Lord. Do not touch what is unclean, and I will receive you" (2 Cor. 6:17, NKJV).

**Serve.** As oysters are served to others, our job is to serve others. We imitate Christ when we serve. There are numerous opportunities to serve, so get involved. Serving benefits others and helps to prepare us for marriage by allowing us to practice placing the needs of someone else ahead of our own. The body of Christ needs whatever it is we have to offer—no service is too small. "As each one has received a gift, minister it to one another, as good stewards of the manifold grace of God" (1 Pet. 4:10, NKJV).

Every Christian single can master the ability to enjoy single living in just a few simple steps. To do so, understand that you are whole and your ability to enjoy life is not contingent on whether you have a mate. Jesus came so that you may have abundant life (John 10:10), so be sure to enjoy every season of it! An oyster's abundant living comes by way of producing a pearl. Pearls are the only precious stones produced by a living thing. They are jewels produced by a life-giving creature. We are also jewels that are the product of a living and life-giving God. We start out tiny and end up becoming the most beautiful natural stones there are. The pearl reminds us that God gave every soaring bird, pretty flower, panoramic mountain vista—and even oyster—to show us things about Him. God's final Word to us is His dear Son, and all that is written of Him, which we should read about in our Bibles—the book of Pearls.

---

"Singles, too, must see the penultimate status of marriage. If single Christians don't develop a deeply fulfilling love relationship with Jesus, they will put too much pressure on their DREAM of marriage, and that will create pathology in their lives as well."

—Timothy Keller, *The Meaning of Marriage: Facing the Complexities of Commitment with the Wisdom of God*

## Life Reflections

Pray for:

- Contentment

- Deliverance from the spirit of loneliness

- Wisdom to deal with the pressure of being single

Consider:

1. What stood out to you in this chapter?

2. What changes will you make as a result of reading this chapter?

# Bumps, Bruises and Blocks

In today's society, singleness is not the easiest lifestyle to live. So many distractions can derail you and break your focus. The weak spots in our armor lead to bumps, bruises, and (road) blocks ("the 3 Bs"). The enemy is always looking for an opening to get his foot in the door. The simple act of you pondering why you are single is enough for him to plant more negative seeds that will alter your mood. Before you know it, such things can consume you. You must be aware of the enemy's tactics and his operation in your life so you can decrease the "3 Bs." Peter wrote the following to the elect exiles scattered abroad in Pontus, Galatia, Cappadocia, Asia, and Bithynia:

> Casting the whole of your care [all your anxieties, all your worries, all your concerns, once and for all] on Him, for He cares for you affectionately *and* cares about you watchfully. Be well balanced (temperate, sober of mind), be vigilant *and* cautious at all times; for that enemy of yours, the devil, roams around like a lion roaring [in fierce hunger], seeking someone to seize upon *and* devour. Withstand him; be firm in faith [against his onset—rooted, established, strong, immovable, and determined], knowing that the same (identical) sufferings are appointed to your brotherhood (the whole body of Christians) throughout the world. (1 Pet 5:7-9, AMP)

We should be disciplined and aware of the spiritual pitfalls coming before us. For example, if your weakness is lusting after the opposite sex, this opportunity will be presented to you. If you struggle with walking in love, an opportunity to be offended will come before you. A strong want for marriage will produce a counterfeit before the real thing. Thus, know your weaknesses and the cracks in your armor. Peter raised the concern and gave the answer. He said, be cautious when Satan rears his head; you can resist him with faith. Satan has three areas in which he will attack. "For all that is in the world—the lust of the flesh [craving for sensual gratification] and the lust of the eyes [greedy longings of the mind] and the pride of life [assurance in one's own resources or in the stability of earthly things]—these do not come from the Father but are from the world [itself]" (1 John 2:16, AMP). The lust of flesh includes tasting, touching, smelling, and hearing. Lust of the eye is seeing. Pride of life entails thinking that you are special because of who you are, what you have, who you know, or what you look like. Loving the world's way of doing things squeezes out loving the Father and isolates you from Him. Bumps, bruises, and (road) blocks come from wanting your own way, wanting everything for yourself, and wanting to appear important. Scripture shows this work on the Mount of Temptation in Matthew 4:1-10 and Luke 4:1-13—Jesus was led into the wilderness by the Holy Spirit, to be tempted by Satan.

## Lust of the Flesh

His first temptation appealed to the lust of the flesh. Jesus had just completed a 40-day fast, and the Bible says He was hungry. The matter is not if the tempter will come, but when. Consider the circumstances that preceded the temptation. Jesus:

- had a devout frame of mind,
- was engaged in public obedience,
- was exceedingly humble,
- was blessed by heavenly assurance,
- was filled with the Holy Spirit, and was completely separated from the world.

> ...the FLESH is filled with a desire to satisfy its shameful appetite, showy appearances, and shallow applause. It will indulge but never be filled.

In this temptation, Satan was not questioning Jesus's divinity; he was challenging Him to prove it through works. Satan doesn't question your Christianity; he challenges your belief and actions to follow. Whether single or married, Christian or non-Christian, you will battle lust of the flesh from time to time. Yielding to lust of the flesh will cause you to misuse what God created for pleasure. What Satan presented to Jesus made sense because His hunger represented human wants. It makes sense for a single person to want a spouse. It makes sense to crave intimacy and acceptance. Nevertheless, are you willing to sacrifice the making of Christ in you to gratify your desires? Lust of the flesh is tricky because it is designed to bring gratification. It is an insatiable craving to satisfy a legitimate desire in an illegitimate way. You can lust after money, possessions, recognition, or sex. I once read that the flesh is filled with a desire to satisfy its shameful appetite, showy appearances, and shallow applause. It will indulge but never be filled.

The times when I engaged in such indulgence, I had opened the door for it. James 1:14 teaches that we are drawn away and enticed by the desires we hide in our hearts. The opportunity is presented, but it is our heart's desire that decides to take action. I remember craving attention from a man; I longed for compliments, affection, and companionship. I met someone who provided all of that for me but he always reminded me that our conversations were private and he would cover me. Yes, they were private conversations, but there is no cover for fulfilling lust of the flesh. Besides, he was the one creating opportunities for me to act on my fleshly desires. I understand that he may have kept it private, but God is all knowing and all seeing. Christian singles ranging in age from 13 to 40 revealed:

Female, Age Range: 13-20

*I accepted Christ and promised myself never to allow the flesh to reign. But after a week, I slipped. After I engaged, I felt the guilt and shame. I attended a youth conference. There I felt the presence of the Lord, but three days after the conference, I fell again. I finally was able to start walking in deliverance when I repented before God and told friends at my Christian school and my parents. I am still tempted from time to time, but it is the goodness of God that led me to repentance.*

Male, Age Range: 13-20

*Striving to please the flesh is an illusion because when you mess up, you can feel your soul crumble. Not just my soul, but also the souls that are linked to me that I am responsible for. I thank God for His strength and for just the Holy Spirit giving me the feeling of conviction that leads me back to His feet for repentance. I have given my testimony and have even confessed to my sister as well. She is helping me through this. So now, I am just claiming my victory, praising God for it, and believing that one day I will lose count of my missed marks.*

## Female, Age Range: 31-40

*One day, I ran into a minister who talked about being free from sin and the lust of the flesh. The victory for me came one day as fear was telling me "you may have stopped for now." But God helped me realize something that I hadn't before, when He told me "you never have to do it again." I never knew I was free from sin and that I had a choice. I have that choice because of Christ, who has made me free from sin. I didn't have to perform every whim of my own sinful desires. Now I've been free for three years. I'm free to talk about it. I thought I'd go to my grave with this sin.*

## Male, Age Range: 31-40

*Yielding to the lust of the flesh with my best friend, I entered into a life of hard drug use and casual relationships. I lost my job and house because I could not pay my bills. I was in a living hell and I felt I had brought it on myself and punishment was my due. Something inside me told me I had to save myself now and turn back. This was the beginning of hope. In the next few months, God began to reach down to me. He wiped my tears as they fell and made me feel His love wrapped around me. I rededicated my life to Him. I began to attend a prayer meeting and seek His Spirit and healing that ONLY He brings. That was a year ago. I am now committed to living in the Spirit and by Faith. I have one desire now, to reach out to those around me who have not discovered the reality of God's Kingdom here on earth, to influence anyone who is in a similar position that I was and to let them know there is another way. A highway of holiness is there and we are free to begin our walk on it in complete freedom from shame, fear, and uncertainty.*

Doing the right thing is a matter of choosing, not feeling. Compromise doesn't only refer to fornication. Compromise entails allowing someone to speak to you in an un-Christ like manner, cross boundaries you set, attack your Godly perspective, cause you to question your position in Christ, or fight for your self-esteem. When you confront someone about how their actions or words affect you and their response resembles, "You must be strong or else I would bulldoze over you," they have no real appreciation for you. We have responsibility for the decisions we make that open the door to others dealing with us unfairly. I once befriended a man who encouraged me to give into his advances although he knew I wanted to do things God's way. At times, I felt like giving in; but I knew doing the right thing was a matter of choosing, not feeling. Until a person develops a greater appreciation for the things of God, he or she will not develop a greater appreciation for people with Godly priorities. There is a huge difference between the natural person and the spiritual person. Thus, your greatest consideration should always be how a person supports you spiritually. Can they handle your emotions with a tender heart? It is one thing for someone to open your heart, but another thing to touch your spirit.

When you give an ear to the world's perspective and way of doing things, you compromise. It is not always the act—sometimes it is the consideration. I am reminded of Psalms 1:1: We should not follow the advice, plans, or purposes of someone who is displaying ungodly character. We should not submit or hang around those engaging in sinful activities. Lastly, we should not relax and rest around someone who is contemptuous. Instead, we should follow the precepts, instructions, and teaching of the Word of God—and ponder them often. Satan will secure his greatest foothold when you are vulnerable to moral attack, criticism, and temptation. As a result of not following Psalms 1:1, compromise takes place. An example is spending time with someone who does not intend to enter into a Christian courtship that could lead to marriage. You must decide to rise above your vulnerability and no longer compromise. Every single person (man and woman) should know their value without wavering. Satan wears out the Saints of the Most High God by working on us. I had made it easy for him. All I could think about was being in my early forties, still single, and having no children. Such thoughts became my life and reality. Living victoriously over the flesh requires evaluation from all angles. If any angle does not line up with the Word of God, do not accept it or compromise. There is no comfort in compromise, no matter how the other person tries to console you. Jesus could have compromised by yielding to Satan's request to fulfill His hunger, but He did not. Always side with the Word of God. No great revelation here, but there is grace for you to make the right decision.

## Pride of Life

Then Satan took Jesus onto the turret of the temple and told Him to throw Himself off so the angels could keep Him. Satan was trying to get Jesus to take a shortcut to the cross. Jesus again responded with the Word. Jesus won because He recognized Satan's mode of attack: appealing to the pride of life. Every person wants God to demonstrate His approval. Two things to note in this temptation: 1. Satan falsely quoted, and 2. Satan wrongly applied the Word of God. Satan's goal was to make Jesus doubt, using the pride of life. Making pride of life a priority will always produce doubt and wavering beliefs. Listening to others and not the Holy Spirit provokes weakness in faith and vacillation in the face of God's promises. The enemy may use a person to create doubt; however, you are responsible for your double mindedness. Doubting puts you in a position of demanding things from God to prove His care and concern for you. From the beginning, Satan has attempted to raise doubts about the honesty and goodness of God. Daily, he still whispers in our ears, "Yea, hath God said?"

Pride of life can be defined as anything that is "of the world," meaning leading to arrogance, pride in self, presumption, and boasting. Its essence offers the illusion of God-like qualities wherein we boast of worldly wisdom. It is the vain craving for honor and applause, or the stubborn mindset that will not allow one to repent and confess sins. As we see, Jesus did not fall to this temptation—but oftentimes we do. The arrogant boasting that makes up pride of life motivates the other two lusts as it seeks to elevate itself above others and fulfill personal desires. It is the root cause of strife in families, churches, and nations. Pride exalts the self in direct contradiction to Jesus's statement that those who follow Him must take up their cross (an instrument of death) and deny themselves. It is the arrogance that separates us from others and limits our effectiveness in the Kingdom. My recent pride of life moment was when I told God I was going to keep my options open on meeting a companion. I was stepping into the realm of helping out God, as though I knew the end from the beginning. As a result, I had to fight the good fight of faith to overcome the emotional baggage of "keeping my options open." God reminded me that was my own doing—I let my cravings for attention decide for me and not my spirit. Although I did not yield to temptation, my spirit was affected. My advice to singles is, do not flirt with temptation or pride of life because it will leave you broken. What others are saying about the pride of life:

Female, Age Range: 21-30

*Sometimes, pride of life can come in a disguise. If the road has been rocky, hard, and grueling, and by the grace of God we survive, we might say to ourselves, "I am tough," "I am a survivor," "I can get through," etc. I didn't recognize the journey that God was taking me through. I did not see how God was walking with me. I did not recognize sin in my life. Thus, I did not repent. For me, I was just grateful that I survived the journey and now I am a survivor, tougher and wiser. Yet the journey may have been about God's outworking in me—cleansing, restoring, and clearing away the debris.*

Male, Age Range: 21-30

*Thinking about what is good for me. Everything had to meet to my standards: Pride in my denomination is one of the worst, for it takes many on the wrong path; pride that God has to meet our standards or we won't follow them—I made God what I wanted Him to be. Pride is our free will, so we can choose because we are not robots. He has to wait for us because we have the last say—not Him. That is pride.*

The cure for minimizing your experiences operating in pride is to embrace humility and build you. Notice I did not say "cut," because on this journey of learning to live victorious as a Christian single, you will make bad decisions. In 2 Peter 1:5-8, we learn that we daily need to add goodness to our faith; knowledge to goodness; self-control to knowledge; perseverance to self-control; godliness to perseverance; brotherly kindness to godliness; and love to brotherly kindness. We must cultivate these characteristics in our lives on a daily basis. They can't be purchased or acquired from the established educational systems, from self, from a self-help book, or from a training course. Our character develops through experience and making the best out of situations God allows in our lives.

> You are **NOT PERFECT** and the Lord does not need you to be. He does require you to be on the road of improving every day and have the heart to develop a *deeper relationship with Him*. ~~~~~~~

Scripture continues, saying that if you live by these qualities in increasing measure, they will keep you from being ineffective and unproductive in your knowledge of the Lord Jesus Christ. You are not perfect and the Lord does not need you to be. He does require you to be on the road of improving every day and have the heart to develop a deeper relationship with Him. As we exercise goodness, knowledge, self-control, perseverance, godliness, kindness, and love to those around us, we will discover the goodness of God and His plan for our lives.

**Lust of the Eye**

Satan took Jesus upon a mountain and showed Him the kingdoms and their glory. Satan took it a step further, promising it all to Jesus if He committed to worship him. This last temptation appealed to the lust of the eye, which always leads to deception. Deception is as a lie—the act of making someone believe something that is not true. It infuses a lie or half-truth to make a deliberate misrepresentation to cheat, blind, or manipulate. Like Jesus, you should always say "No" to deception. Many times, as singles, we struggle with seeing what is real versus what is counterfeit. For those who live in the light of the cross, deception is Satan's effective tool. Through deception, he can push you to a lifestyle of sin, fear, and unbelief. When it comes to the lust of the eye, things are never what they appear. Being a Christian single from my late twenties to now, I have gone through many seasons of comparing myself to others, causing me to grow weary at times.

I recall turning 40 and becoming concerned that I was still single. At that point, I was recovering from a broken ankle, agitated that I had no husband to care for me daily. I was open to a relationship, but realizing the world of dating had changed left me confused. Needless to say, I began to believe the deception that everyone was married or in a relationship—except me. I became obsessed with watching couples and comparing myself to the women I saw. Comparing my size, looks, hair, clothes, smile, make-up; and such opened up the greatest level of vulnerability a woman could experience. This went on for years, until I took a solo trip to Dallas for my 43rd birthday. I began to watch couples while I was sitting in a restaurant having dinner. Yes, I was gearing up to start the comparison game. But that day, God had a different plan in mind. Just as I was venturing down my usual road, God said, "Look again," and He allowed the scales to fall of my eyes. Spiritually, I saw broken men and women: men and women uncommitted to each other; men sitting with women but watching other women; many games, manipulations, and controlling spirits. At once, I said, "God, I do not want to live like this." These couples appeared to be happy, but at that moment, God exposed their hearts to me, revealing something different. I decided not to believe the deception Satan was putting before me. "But of these who seemed to be somewhat, (whatsoever they were, it maketh no matter to me: God accepteth no man's person) for they who seemed to be somewhat in conference added nothing to me" (Gal. 2:6, KJV). This writer is saying: Stop comparing yourself to others! It will not add any new requirements to you because God is not impressed—so you should not be either.

*"For those who live in the light of the cross, deception is Sa-tan's effective tool."*

"Your eyes are windows into your body. If you open your eyes wide in wonder and belief, your body fills up with light. If you live squinty-eyed in greed and distrust, your body is a dank cellar. If you pull the blinds on your windows, what a dark life you will have!" (Matt. 6:22-23, MSG). The lust of the eyes is when the eye notices things it wants and doesn't have. It may be things or people, but in either case, we must avoid it because it comes not from the Father but from the world. In The Forerunner Commentary, John W. Ritenbaugh described worldliness as the love of beauty without a corresponding love of righteousness. This is correct. It comes right out of the "original sin" story told in Genesis 3:6. Eve saw that the fruit was good for food, pleasant to the eyes, and something to be desired. These three references concern the appeal of beauty. As the record shows, Adam and Eve did not love righteousness. The love of beauty and the pull of temptation are inextricably entwined. Almighty God made you to love beauty and to seek it out, even though no one's notion of beauty is the same.

**Do you LOVE righteousness more than you LOVE what you see and desire with your eyes?**

Ritenbaugh further wrote that beauty is being used in a very broad sense as a term for things that are appealing and have the power to create want within us. Thus, we want things we consider beautiful. The problem is that, like Adam and Eve, we do not have a corresponding love of righteousness. We will break the laws of God to have what we consider beautiful. Sometimes people commit vicious evils to have what they find appealing and beautiful at the time. Beauty delights the senses, gratifies, and evokes admiration and excitement within a person. Therein lies its danger; it does not matter in what one finds delight. The result of having a love of beauty without a corresponding love of righteousness leads to abuse. Adam and Eve were kicked out of the Garden of Eden, the most beautiful spot on earth, because they did not love righteousness. This is a simple yet powerful lesson! The beauty was there to behold—even the beauty of the forbidden fruit—luring them. Did God put it there to tempt them into sin? No! He put it there for them to admire and bring glory to the Creator God in their rightful use of it. Instead, they abused their privilege because they did not love righteousness, and the beauty was taken away from them. Do you love righteousness more than you love what you see and desire with your eyes?

Christians have always been, and will always be, lured by the same three temptations. Satan doesn't change his methods, because they continue to be successful. He tempts us with the lust of the flesh—sexual gratification, gluttony, excessive alcohol consumption, and drugs (both legal and illegal), as well as, the deeds of the flesh. Paul warned the Galatians about sexual immorality, impurity, sensuality, idolatry, sorcery, enmity, strife, jealousy, fits of anger, rivalries, dissensions, divisions, envy, drunkenness, orgies, and things like these. Satan uses the lust of the eyes—the endless accumulation of "stuff" with which we fill our homes and garages, and the insatiable desire for more, better, and newer possessions that ensnare us and harden our hearts to the things of God. But Satan's most evil temptation is the pride of life, the very sin that resulted in his expulsion from heaven. He desired to be God, not to serve God. Pride of life comes not from the Father, but from the world—and it passes away with the world. But those who resist and overcome the temptation of pride of life do the will of God, and the man who does the will of God lives forever.

---

"God wants you to be delivered from what you have done and from what has been done to you—both are equally important to Him."

—Joyce Meyer, *Beauty for Ashes: Receiving Emotional Healing*

## Life Reflections

Pray for:

- Deliverance from lust of the flesh, lust of the eye, and pride of life

- Revelation of what is real versus what is counterfeit

- Development in righteousness

- An accountability partner

Consider:

1. What struggles do you have with lust of the flesh, lust of the eye, and pride of life?

2. Write down one thing you will do to overcome each area.

# CHAPTER 3

# Broken Made Whole

As we read 2 Samuel 13, the story never goes on to tell us what happened to Tamar or how she felt after being raped. But, we can guess that she had feelings of hurt, anger, hate, betrayal, low self-worth, and guilt.

- Hurt—because someone Tamar knew had hurt her and she could not understand why.
- Anger—because her father, the king, did nothing to avenge her.
- Hate—because in a time where virginity was valued, she no longer had hers to *give* to someone in marriage.
- Betrayal—because she trusted and was then disappointed.
- Self-worth—because now she wonders who will want a messed-up, used, and degraded individual such as herself.

Have you walked in Tamar's shoes? Are you alive but emotionally broken? Tired of living a half-life, a life of the memories and pain—hurt? Take authority over every issue that hinders you from walking in wholeness. Wholeness is not what others lend you; it is what you create for yourself with the help of the Holy Spirit. I have ministered to countless singles who felt they were less than 100% and allowed their belief to dictate their direction in life. They put off life desires, waiting for someone else—besides God—to make them whole. News flash: as a single or as a married person, you are responsible for allowing God—and not others—to frame your world. Being *whole* is a positive and healthy level of being and doing. Wholeness refers to your mind, body, and soul; to social, material, and cultural aspects. Wholeness brings about a freedom and confidence that others cannot give you. It involves continuously examining yourself and seeking ways to improve in life.

Brokenness describes a person who is discouraged and unhappy. Often, the person feels crushed and bitter. Psalm 34:18 describes the brokenhearted and crushed person as having been kicked in the gut. God wants you WHOLE; complete; nothing missing, nothing broken—physically, spiritually, emotionally, mentally, and financially. Christian wholeness and Christian brokenness are incompatible. Every Christian should employ everything that Jesus has done to make us whole in every way. Even though Christians may remain broken in life, no Christian should be content with such state of living.

> God wants you **WHOLE;** complete; nothing missing, nothing broken—physically, spiritually, emotionally, mentally, and financially.

God doesn't break you so that He can make you whole, any more than you break your child's leg so you can nurse them back to health! Brokenness occurs when we try to live life on our terms and come up empty. The Bible is full of examples of people with broken lives because they tried to follow God while living according to their own plans. Shattered dreams and broken lives empower us to see what is wrong with our lives as we gain new insight into ourselves. When plans fail and dreams shatter, we see the wrong in our lives. It is then that we realize our insensitivity to God. Jacob knew God's plan to fulfill His promise to Abraham's descendants, but Jacob implemented his own plan to make it happen by cheating his twin brother Esau out of his birthright. Jacob fled with the clothes on his back and a stone for a pillow. It was in his brokenness that God appeared and reaffirmed His promise to Abraham. During Abraham's wandering, he lied about Sarah being his wife—trusting in his ability to offer safety. He was tired of waiting for the promised son, so he fathered a son by his wife's servant. Paul had issues because he persecuted Christians, and Judas betrayed Jesus for money. Brokenness ushers in feelings of shame, frustration, confusion, fear, and spiritual warfare. Out of our natural curiosity, we try to figure out why something is broken. We are taught to work harder to overcome our brokenness; we end up going in circles, unwilling to face the real issue. We are like Jacob and Abraham; we work longer, harder, better—we try to be more ingenious so we can fix our own problems. Satan uses brokenness for bad, but God for our good.

Life brokenness resembles a broken (fractured) bone in our bodies. Bones are tough stuff—but even tough stuff can break. Like a wooden pencil, bones will bend under strain. But with too much or sudden pressure, bones snap. Breaking a bone shocks the whole body. Amazingly, God created the body to heal itself, but even in the best of cases, fractures often need medical attention to heal. After the break, the body attempts to put itself back together again. To make sure the bone heals, doctors must first diagnose the fracture and its severity. They align and immobilize the fractured bone. The patient may need traction for more complex fractions, to keep the alignment. Fractures might need surgery to remove foreign material, bone fragments, or to insert something (rod, pin, or screw) to stabilize the bone while it heals. Then, the patient needs rehabilitation to increase muscle mass, strength, and flexibility for the healed limb. The same thing that occurs in the natural realm happens in the spiritual realm. No matter how tough you are, you are subject to brokenness when life pressures take their toll. When that happens, you have to confront or diagnose the issue(s) leading to the brokenness, align your life with God by removing what is not like Him, and allow God to rehabilitate you. I know what people mean when they say that a Christian should become "broken." They mean bringing the body (flesh) and soul (mind, will, and emotions) under the control of the Spirit. Renewal of the mind is the start to becoming whole!

Many of us experience brokenness due to the words and actions of others towards us, strongholds we developed, and soul ties we create. Every time someone criticizes us (constructively, unconstructively, warranted, or unwarranted), they sow a seed or plant a thought. Every seed has potential to land, grow, take root, or die. There is an old saying that we tend to criticize others by their actions and ourselves by our intentions. Most criticism is given to find fault or to condemn. The person with a critical spirit tends to dwell on the negative and seek to point it out to us. If we are not careful, their pointing out our flaws can cause brokenness in us. I remember a person who always pointed out a flaw before giving a compliment—the flaw or fault always came before the positive or encouragement. Whether a person is criticizing your house décor or layout, the clothes you wear, the food you cook, or the lifestyle you live, the outcome can be brokenness.

When others are very critical of you or your lifestyle, they are striving to weaken your position and strengthen theirs as a way of dealing with brokenness in their own lives. We singles seek advice from those who can guide us—but if wholeness is our goal, the person with a critical spirit does not have the answer. Instead, surround yourself with those who build you up—and not those who tear you down. Ever had a guest who did not hold their tongue regarding things they did not like about your house? Whether it was the color of paint on your wall, your furniture, or the tidiness of your house, they came ready to size you up and judge. A critical person always looks for ways to discredit you or prove the opposite of what you tell or show them. In most cases, that person is fighting for their own self-esteem and will put you in a position to fight for yours. Other causes of criticism are their insecurity, immaturity, unrenewned mind—and Satan himself. We all have areas in our lives that need work; none will reach the point of perfection on earth. We need either deliverance or to learn how to manage such areas better.

God positioned us to break out from and through things, so we can break into what He has designed for us. To break out is to emerge from a restrictive condition. When breaking through, we overcome or penetrate obstacles. To break into something new, we train, adapt for the purpose, or begin suddenly. Before you can start breaking out, you must know yourself and be honest about the areas in which you fall short. Why is honesty so hard?

Female, Age Range 21-30

*When we are honest with ourselves, we have to admit that we are not perfect. In ways, I labeled myself as inferior to others. None of us is quick to admit that we are wrong. This lead to pride standing in our way. It is freeing as a Christian to admit faults and shortcomings.*

Male, Age Range 21-30

*Honesty is hard because having insecurities can make one anxious. Being honest requires the ability to see yourself and to be confident with what you see. Not everyone can do that.*

Female, Age Range 41-50

*It was difficult for me to accept who I was. I had issues of past embarrassments and managing my private emotions. I always say, "Never lie to yourself or you may end up lying to others."*

Male, Age Range 41-50

*For me, I needed a tiny bit of a lie to give me confidence to keep going and trust what I was doing. Right or wrong, I did it.*

I see brokenness every time I am in the presence of a grieving family. I see brokenness when I visit people in hospitals or seniors' residences. I see brokenness in human relationships. Former friends who could not see eye-to-eye and it drove them apart. Marriage relationships everywhere under stress and breaking under the strain. I see brokenness in my own life. Day after day, I am reminded of my own failures and imperfections. Brokenness can take many forms. It may include insignificance, emptiness, excessive anxiety, bitterness, depression, addiction, persistent shame, obsessive thoughts, compulsive behavior, and even perfectionism. People who suffer from perfectionism cannot live up to their own expectations. Some try to overcome pain by filling their lives with substitutes. These substitutes include alcohol, drugs, sex, material things, and even work. The main idea is to numb the pain with something else and to avoid pain with these substitutes. Most substitutes increase feelings of brokenness and hopelessness, and lead to lower self-esteem. In short, you want to please others even if it means denying basic issue(s) about yourself.

Truth is difficult to face if you know people in your circle will find it hard to accept. Today, I'm not afraid to admit my shortcomings. However, this was not always the case. At 26, I moved away to a new city—away from my friends and family. I spent time alone, getting to know me and discovering I looked good on the outside but needed work on the inside. As I pulled away the layers, I saw that I had lived my life to decrease my flaws and play up my positive attributes. I'm here to tell you, 17 years later, I'm still pulling away the layers. It wasn't until God started to work in my life that I began self-evaluate. My real problems with pride, control, being spoiled, and other issues led me on this journey of transparency. God showed me insecurities that had been with me since my twenties. Do you know you can bury things instead of overcoming them? When God shows you, it's time for you to start moving toward deliverance. You and I will always be works in progress! A wise woman once said to me, "When what others do irritates you, it's because you do those same things." I realized some of my brokenness came from other's criticism, but I was also causing brokenness by my self-criticism. Are you causing brokenness because of your critical spirit? We criticize because of our own selfish interests. For example, we sometimes become critical when comparing ourselves to those around us. We try to find fault in others to prove that we are smarter, better looking, happier, or wealthier. We are critical when others fail to do what we ask or do not do what we think is right. A family member, friend, or co-worker who fails to meet our expectations can lead us to a critical attitude. Even our own frustrations can lead to such an attitude. If life is not turning out the way we wish, we hide our own frustrations by finding fault with others. Jesus said not to judge "so that you will not be judged" (Matt. 7:1, NASB).

Jesus then explained why a judgmental attitude is so dangerous: "For in the way you judge, you will be judged; and by your standard of measure, it will be measured to you" (Matt. 7:2, NASB). When we judge, we invite judgment upon ourselves. The Bible says that judgment will be merciless to one who has shown no mercy. By judging others, we hide our own hypocrisy. In John 8, religious leaders brought a woman who had sexual sin to Jesus; the leaders wanted to kill her. Jesus responded, if any of you have never sinned, then go ahead and throw the first stone at her. Nobody threw one. God alone reserves the right to judge each person. Apostle Paul said we should not attempt revenge, because God is our avenger. The cure for criticism is understanding the nature of God's judgment. Regardless of how good we think we are, our righteous deeds are as a filthy garment. We cannot make up for the things we have done. Left alone, we still deserve God's judgment. If we understood the judgment that we each deserve from God, we would stop criticizing others. From now on, follow Jesus's instruction to take a close look at your own life first. You may even discover why you are so critical of others. The faults of others are often obvious to us. During these times, we need to make sure we give grace instead. Thank God for others and pray for blessing and revelation in their lives. God has granted you mercy. He has paid the debt for your sins. Now, the only debt you owe is to offer His love and mercy to others, for "mercy triumphs over judgment" (James 2:13; NASB). If we lift ourselves out of brokenness and try to become whole without turning to God, we will fail and remain critical. We may be able to improve in life, but complete wholeness is not possible.

We must turn to our Creator for help. He alone has the complete answer for us. Given this, let us begin our search for God, for He is the King of mending broken hearts. Indeed, because of His love, He is searching for us! He wants us to respond. Jesus said, "I am come that they might have life, and that they might have it more abundantly" (John 10:10, KJV). Here, Jesus stated His goal. He wants us to have abundant life. This abundant life does not always shield us from brokenness, but it will help us through the dark seasons and give us victory. The Psalmist (147:3) said, He would heal your broken hurt and bind up your wounds. Jesus is always present to heal our suffering hearts and treat our wounds. He will give us abundant life! To overcome our brokenness, we must realize that a power greater than ourselves must heal us. Alone, we cannot make the journey from brokenness to wholeness. Jesus will not impose His healing upon us. We must make the decision to turn to Him for healing. Becoming whole can be both painful and exhilarating; it takes time, courage, and faith. In my studies, I found these Seven Secrets to Healing Brokenness of body, mind, and spirit:

> *Embrace* your personal value. *Believe* that you are worthy of time, effort, and investment to become whole.

1.  **Awareness**. Acknowledge the fractures in your life. Recognize signs of brokenness—swelling, sadness, numbness, and ache. Denial delays fulfillment; in this case, healing.

2.  **Worthiness**. Embrace your personal value. Believe that you are worthy of time, effort, and investment to become whole. Nurture your mind with positive thoughts; your body with nutritious food; and your spirit with love.

3.  **Willingness**. Exercise discipline. To be renewed, you must be willing to do the hard work facing you; coming back requires a mix of intention and sweat.

4.  **Readiness**. Prepare for the healing. Reach out for the support. Spiritual sit-ups will strengthen the core muscles of faith in God. You can do this!

5. **Forgiveness**. Let go of the resentment, guilt, and anger. The Gospels offer counsel on the difficult task of forgiving those who have caused us harm. Begin with self-forgiveness.

6. **Fearlessness**. Dare to venture outside your comfort zone. This may mean disregarding stigma, making lifestyle changes, developing new friendships, and forming new habits. This is not easy stuff. To paraphrase the words of a world leader who came from a "broken" home, there is audacity in hope.

7. **Gratefulness**. Express appreciation. If you envision wholeness—see it; imagine the experience of wholeness—taste it; believe in the possibility of wholeness—touch it; and thank God for the coming transformation—hear it. You will start healing. Celebrate.

(Taken from Mental and Emotional Wellness Solutions by Maxine Bigby Cunningham, Chief Visionary of Empowered Walking Enterprise/Ministries LLC, www.empoweredwalking ministries.com)

I once purchased from a high-end store a beautiful planter for my front porch. To preserve it, I brought it indoors every winter. One winter, I forgot to bring it into the garage. When I realized it, it was already subzero weather, windy and snowing. The wind blew the pot over; it broke in two pieces. I had hopes of gluing it together, so I attempted to put it in the garage. Just as I stepped into the garage with the planter, it slipped out of my hand. I tried to catch it, but it fell and shattered on the garage floor. A sound echoed in my heart: you just broke this one-of-a-kind planter. As I stared at the pieces, I realized that I was like the planter. Either through my own fault or through someone else's, I was broken. I picked up the pieces and put them in a pile. Now, I had only a pile of broken pieces. I began to get upset, but that did not help. The planter was still broken—no frustration, anger, tears, or beating myself up would ever put it (or myself) back together again. There was no more emotion left; just emptiness. I thought I could glue it back together again with the "right" glue. You, like the planter, were just a pile of broken pieces, emotionless. But you have a Creator—a loving, caring God who knows you and knew you in your mother's womb. He made you.

A potter would know the best way to repair planters because he or she created them. God, who created you, knows the best way to repair you. He is the glue. He knows how to put you together so that you are stronger and less likely to break again. I decided to get the planter fixed, so I collected the pieces and took it to a potter. He took the pieces from me and began to reassemble the planter before my eyes. It is the same way with Jesus. He sees that you are broken and knows you cannot cry anymore; you have nothing left to give. God is waiting for you to give Him permission to start picking up your pieces and putting you back together. It may take a while for you to feel differently. To become whole, you need to rest in your Maker's hands and trust that He can pick up your pieces. He knows where they need to go and how to bind them together. As the potter is the expert to fix a shattered planter, your Creator is the expert to put you back together. Hold God to those promises; read them, repeat them. Remind Him daily. He will strengthen you and keep you. You will be as a cedar in Lebanon: Strong; from broken to whole; a new you!

"God uses broken things. It takes broken soil to produce a crop, broken clouds to give rain, broken grain to give bread, broken bread to give strength. It is the broken alabaster box that gives forth perfume. It is Peter, weeping bitterly, who returns to greater power than ever."

—Vance Havner

## Life Reflections

Pray for:

- Restoration and preparation

- Forgiveness

- Those who caused your brokenness

- Those you caused to be broken

- Wholeness and a renewed mind

Consider:

1. What has caused your brokenness?

2. What is your immediate plan to overcome brokenness?

# CHAPTER 4

# Breaking of Day

Once upon a time, there was a tortoise on a ship that sank. Sometime later, the tortoise made it to a desert land surrounded by water on all sides except for one. The landward side led up to a big, steep, craggy mountain. To avoid starving to death, the tortoise decided to climb to the top of the mountain, hoping to cross to the other side. When he got to the snow-covered summit, it was freezing; then a blizzard started. He managed just to make out a small pathway leading to the other side of the mountain. Then a monster appeared, guarding the path and shouting loudly. Such a sight filled the tortoise with fright. Looking around, he saw many other animals lying frozen to death with looks of horror on their faces. But the tortoise didn't go into his shell. Instead, he summoned his courage to move ahead on the path toward the monster. The closer the tortoise got, the more the monster changed its shape. When he was upon it, the tortoise realized what he thought was a monster was a great pile of rocks shaped as a monster. As for the shouting, it was just the sound of the wind blowing through a small cave. The tortoise descended into a beautiful valley filled with woods and plenty of food. He lived there and became known everywhere as the Brave Little Tortoise.

The tortoise had to break through and out of several issues. He was fearful that he might starve or freeze to death or be killed by a monster. He could have allowed these issues to hinder his progress, but he decided to overcome and not be self-centered. When he made the decision to act in courage, he realized what he feared was only an illusion of what could be. Like the tortoise, illusions in our lives cloud our vision and hinder our progress daily. We are subject to life circumstances in our state of being single. For example, I might have said, "I can afford to go shopping because it's just me." This statement demonstrates that I was self-centered. Single people can easily fall into this trap because they do not have to share. I often hear stories of singles struggling to keep a sense of understanding toward others. Personally, I did not see the problem with this until someone pointed it out to me. Singles do not take the time to understand others' points of view or feelings. Self-centered people are not always easy to identify because they can be personable and kind. Nine times out of ten, the self-centered adult was a spoiled child. A spoiled child cries until the caregiver delivers what the child wants. Spoiled adults expect someone to respond to their cries. When children cry, their needs are met without question; they expect such from life as adults. Spoiled children can become helpless adults and expect the world to adjust to what suits them.

Factors such as being the only child or, in my case, the youngest, lend to these learned behaviors. My eldest sister told me they became poor when I born, meaning the family's attention, focus, and resources were contingent upon what I wanted. I could never change my birth position in the family, so I had to change my mindset. Unbelievably, I am still learning the depth of my personality.

"Selfish" and "self-centered" mean different things to me:

- Selfish: Giving myself priority over others when deciding between the two. For example, selfishness asks, "Should I take that last donut or offer it to someone else? Ah, I'll take it."
- Self-centered: Giving myself priority over others by ignoring them. For example, self-centeredness asks, "Should I have coffee with that last donut?"

Selfish decisions are blatant, deliberate attempts to improve ourselves at the expense of others. No one else might see how deliberate these decisions are, but you know because you struggle with them. Self-centered is more about direction (or mindset) than individual decisions. Ignorance of others is often so pervasive we do not even notice it. We do not even realize that what we are doing is wrong.

Overall, there is a lot of overlap between being selfish and being self-centered. I like to distinguish between them because it helps confront the issues. I am still sorting out how to best work through them, but in general...

- The key to killing selfishness is support.
- The key to killing self-centeredness is awareness.

When considering how to live the victorious life as a single, you must try to overcome issues that interfere in current and future relationships, not to mention how self-centeredness influences our relationship to our Lord and Savior Jesus Christ. To overcome self means to conquer one's own selfish pride. Self-centered pride prevents a soul from being ready and willing to obey God. It blocks out obedience to Christ and blocks souls from even seeking Christ. The suggestion is not to eliminate personality but to enhance it. For example, the twelve apostles chosen by Jesus had different talents and temperaments. Nevertheless, when Jesus was finished with them, (except for Judas Iscariot) they each overcame their clumsy, selfish ambitions and were ready to work their unique talents for the Savior with one mind. "Reprove not a scorner, lest he hate you; reprove a wise man, and he will love you. Give instruction to a wise man and he will be yet wiser; teach a righteous man (one upright and in right standing with God) and he will increase in learning. The reverent and worshipful fear of the Lord is the beginning (the chief and choice part) of Wisdom, and the knowledge of the Holy One is insight and understanding" (Prov. 9:8-10, AMP). In Acts 2:36-42, 3,000 people received the word of truth and then obeyed. It was time for them to crucify self to overcome and obey Christ. Question: Just what did they obey? Answer: the pristine Gospel of Christ. That meant first-century, pure gospel teaching of one body, before Satan had filled humanity with confusion, corruption, dilution, double talk, and sectarianism (and then blamed it on Jesus).

No one is immune to selfishness. A quick glance at biblical examples shows the problem in the called and uncalled alike. We see it in Cain's words about Abel, Nabal's refusal of food to David, Haman's selfish conceit, James and John's seeking high positions, and the priest and Levite's passing by the wounded man. Human nature is self-centered, and we

*When considering how to live the VICTORIOUS LIFE as a single, you must try to overcome issues that interfere in current and future relationships, not to mention how self-centeredness influences our relationship to our Lord and Savior Jesus Christ.*

must overcome it. It manifests by way of self-preservation. People are inclined to hoard. Although hoarding may make a person materially wealthy, it leads to spiritual destitution. We can see selfishness in false ministers who disregard the spiritual health of their flocks while seeking their own pleasures. Ignoring the rights of others, neglecting the needy and suffering, and showing heartless indifference are symptoms of selfishness. In the case of Judas Iscariot, this led to the ultimate selfish act—betrayal of our Savior. Paul wrote that in the last days, selfishness would appear as self-love, self-seeking, and selfish ambition at an unprecedented level. Some do not reciprocate loving deeds; they see not what they have received but what they could get. Selfishness is having too much concern with one's own welfare or interests and too little or no concern for others. We often refer to this person as self-centered, self-absorbed, and self-serving.

God has designed into His law natural ramifications for selfishness. It carries inherent curses, as do other sins. Selfishness results in poverty, sin, and loss of spirituality. Galatians 5:16 discloses a rule about overcoming the propensities of our selfishness and avoiding the evils of strife and contention. If we yield to the power of the Holy Spirit, we can overcome our human tendencies; but because we resist the Spirit, selfishness overcomes us. Paul wrote of the best way to overcome selfishness: "Whatever you do, do all to the glory of God." Throughout his ministry, Paul sought not his own profit but to help others prepare for God's Kingdom. Christ's example—His sacrifice for us—is the ultimate unselfish act. Since selfishness is the seeking of our own lusts,—regardless of its impact on others—sin must be overcome. We must avoid seeking our own pleasures; instead, seek the good of others and put Christ first. This will manifest true Christian love, which "suffers long and is kind," and "does not seek its own."

I have not met a single or married person who did not struggle with self-centeredness or selfishness. Both cause people to focus on themselves, preventing them from experiencing the joys of sharing, giving, and having genuine good quality relationships. Here are things that you can do to try to overcome selfishness:

- Change your mindset. Decide to think and focus on others and not yourself. Self-focus prevents you from establishing and experiencing true, genuine relationships.
- Understand the importance of honoring people as opposed to revering things or money over people. Know that people, and good and genuine

relationships, are more important and more valuable than money and material possessions. Start giving to the poor, widows, and orphans via organizations and charities that help the needy. Giving is one way to combat selfishness.

- Be sensitive to the needs of people around you, in your environment. Discern who may be in need of your help, reach out to them in a caring manner, and help them. This will help to keep the focus off "self" alone, which will help you be a whole, healthy person emotionally, mentally, and spiritually.

We have noticed how people who always think of their own pleasures and interests often make others yield to them. They obtain everything they seek—except happiness—and are always dissatisfied. Our society fuels this in children from infancy. Before you overcome being self-centered, you must consider the driving forces of such behavior. You may say, "I just have high self-esteem—I'm not self-centered." Having self-esteem and being self-centered are two very different things. Self-esteem is one's view of oneself. For example, people with low self-esteem often view themselves in a negative way; hence, the classic low self-esteem symptoms of depression, attention-seeking behavior, passivity, and so forth. Self-centered behaviors are marked by the "me mentality." People who are self-centered often also have low self-esteem: because they are trying to please themselves over others. A person with high self-esteem does not need to be self-centered; they know they are wonderful. People with high self-esteem are easy to get along with: not clingy, confrontational, or selfish. They are the confident people who exist in our lives. Fear and anxiety causes one to pass self-centeredness off as something else.

Fear and self-centeredness play out in ways we sometimes do not often consider. For example, some people may have a strange feeling that they are the butt of an elaborate inside joke. This fear (or paranoia) plays out in their head, telling them there is something wrong with them that they don't recognize, and that their friends are playing a joke on them. They may think that everyone knows they feel ugly and laughs at them behind their backs. But, this person might actually have the most caring and amazing friends who are full of love and have no reason to trick him or her. At times, I have felt this way. Self-reflection made me ponder why I felt the way I did when evidence indicated otherwise. The answer was I had a strong self-centeredness. For me to grow this conspiracy, I must have believed that I was the central figure in many people's lives. This was just not true. People loved me but they did not think and act based on my life. My life is not The Truman Show. I will not even begin to venture a guess as to whether this is nature or nurture, but I have seen others show actions that displays this paranoia. People say or act as if the behavior, thoughts, and philosophies of another person are a direct reflection or attack on their own life.

As a Christian single, fear and anxiety are emotions to be conquered. Active fear and anxiety in your life causes you to lose your identity as a man or woman, and in God. They are both thieves; they will rob from you the greatness God wants you to have. Fear is that uneasiness or apprehension you feel about something. The top three fears for a single person are the fear of rejection, fear of being vulnerable, and fear of change. The latter two were fears I had to overcome. Fear will prevent you from taking faith-filled risks or counting the costs. Fear begins to develop when you internalize what others believe you should be doing. I can recall starting my business: the things people said could have caused me to be fearful of stepping out. Now, 12 years later, I am still in business and prospering. The fear of human opinion (rejection) disables but trusting in God protects you.

*There is a struggle in this Christian life, not with God but with the devil and his lies. If you refuse to fight, you lose.*

Fear is not shameful; it is there to mature you. You should discuss what you fear and why you are fearful with people you trust. On the other hand, anxiety is a high-strung nervousness. It shows that you have a treasure you are concerned about losing. If the treasure you stored up is of earthly things, then you will always be anxious. "Therefore I tell you, stop being perpetually uneasy (anxious and worried) about your life, what you shall eat or what you shall drink, or about your body, what you shall put on. Is not life greater [in quality] than food, and the body [far above and more excellent] than clothing?" (Matt. 6:25, AMP). Being anxious is not going to provoke the hand of God in your life. Instead, it will cause you to build your own house and rely on your own abilities—and to be self-centered.

Anxiety and fear may produce similar responses, but they are different emotions. Anxiety comes from the feeling of a threat, and fear from the emotional response to the threat. Whether real or imagined, anxiety and fear are related and can be the cause of each other. To both, you must take the fight-or-flight approach. God never told us to fight fear and anxiety, just for faith. "Fight on for

God. Hold tightly to the eternal life that God has given you and that you have confessed with such a ringing confession before many witnesses" (1 Tim. 6:12, TLB). There is a struggle in this Christian life, not with God but with the devil and his lies. If you refuse to fight, you lose. Acceptance but not indulgence is the key to overcoming. For me, two out of four of Molly Gordon's principles for overcoming fear and anxiety (i.e., Principles 1 and 3) were most helpful. Evidence proved that fear and anxiety were the roots of my self-centeredness. I recommend that you read one principle at a time and do the exercises in each section before moving to the next one. I also recommend keeping a getting-free-from-fear-and-anxiety journal for 21 days.

### Dealing with Fear and Anxiety:

### Principle 1—FEAR

Redefining FEAR

Knowing that you have a choice about how to deal with your fears, consider the following reframing. Think of FEAR as an acronym for Fantasy Expectations Appearing Real. FEAR takes unsupported premises about impending doom, amplifies them, and presents the alleged results as inevitable failure. Next time you have a fear attack, imagine a big hot-air balloon touching down near you. Notice how tempting it is to grab onto (or even to climb into) the basket, and then see yourself deciding to let it go. Watch the balloon careening over the landscape, while you remain, safe and sound, on the ground.

Dealing with Fear: Exercise

Make a list of your fears, writing as fast as you can to block your internal censor. Include EVERY fear, no matter how small or irrational. Then read the list aloud, suspending judgment. Allow yourself to feel the fear without grabbing on-to the hot-air balloon. Notice that being afraid does not have to mean losing ground.

If it feels comfortable, share your list with a friend. Before sharing your list, explain that you want a witness; that you are practicing how to acknowledge your fears without them pulling you off center. Be clear that you are not asking for help and that you do not need advice. You do not need to be "fixed." Ask your friend to listen and to acknowledge you for being conscious of your fears.

## Dealing with Fear and Anxiety:
## Principle 3—Discern Two Types of Fear

When dealing with fear, realize that not every fear is created equal. In their book, Inner Skiing, W. Timothy Gallwey and Robert Kriegel devoted an entire chapter to two kinds of fear, which they called Fear 1 and Fear 2.

Fear 1 magnifies danger and vulnerability while minimizing your sense of competence. In other words, Fear 1 is Fantasy Expectations Appearing Real. It paralyzes us and prevents action.

Fear 2 mobilizes your whole being for effective action. It includes a series of marvelous physiological changes that prepare the body for peak performance. It focuses attention, provides adrenaline for extraordinary effort, and sharpens perception. Fear 2 promotes effective action.

Identifying Fears: Exercise

Return to the list of fears that you made in the first exercise in this guide. Now you have the opportunity to sort your fears. Work through your list, labeling each fear as:

Fear 1,

Fear 2, or

Not sure, or includes aspects of both types of fear.

If you have not yet written a fear list, do so now. Recording your fears is a powerful step to deal with and manage fears and anxiety. Until you write them down, they are vehicles in gridlock. Once you have them on paper, you can park and move them, clearing a space for forward movement. In this way, writing down your fears creates a space for awareness and choice. (Tip: Refrain from judging yourself or your fears. Just list and label them.)

### Making the Distinction between Two Types of Fear

Once you have a list, notice where Fear 1 and Fear 2 show up. The following distinctions will help:

- Fear 1 promotes panic and confusion; Fear 2 promotes clarity and purpose.
- Fear 1 is often about saving face; Fear 2 is about stepping out of our comfort zones.
- Fear 1 triggers avoidance of the facts; Fear 2 heightens awareness and perception.
- Fear 1 wants us just to stop; Fear 2 wants us to move forward powerfully and safely.
- Fear 1 magnifies danger and vulnerability; Fear 2 calls on our capacity to respond to danger.
- Fear 1 originates in our ego minds; Fear 2 is a whole-system response.

Both types of fear are present in many situations. It is important to use your powers of assessment and discrimination to turn down the volume on Fear 1, while calling on Fear 2 for focus to move forward. With practice, you can transform Fear 1 into Fear 2 by focusing and assessing the real risk and your real competence. For example, Fear 1 makes a terrified skier see a shear drop where the slope is only moderate. When the skier stops and measures the actual slope by holding her pole parallel to it, she increases her awareness of actual conditions and reduces the influence of Fear 1. By continuing to examine the slope, seeing in her mind's eye how she would ski the slope if she chose to, she further reduces panic. When at last she takes off down the hill, trusting in her competence and in her assessment of the challenge, she completes her shift from Fear 1 (panic) into Fear 2 (concentrated exhilaration). Learning to cope with fear in this manner takes practice. The payoff is unlimited as you remove barriers to learning, performance, and joy.

God has not given us a spirit of fear, but many Christians have received a spirit of fear at some time in their lives. They received what was handed out to them. Many times, they received it before they became Christians, and they have not known God well enough to get rid of it since then. In fact, the Bible tells us in 1 John 4:18 that "perfect love casts out fear." The more divine love of God that we receive into our lives, the less scope for fear to get a grip. A man was once robbing a bank. In the midst of it, a woman came up to him and told him to put down the gun. What gave this woman such tremendous courage? She was the man's mother, and her love for her son overcame her sense of fear. Fear tends to attract evil upon us, just as faith tends to attract the goodness and blessings of God. It is the substance of things we hope will not happen—it is faith in reverse because whether you know it or not, we are putting faith in Satan. God wants Christians to be free of such fear. The only good and clean fear is fear of the Lord. Many blessings are associated with the healthy fear of the Lord. We are not talking about that fear here. Nor are we talking about the natural healthy fear that affects us if, for example, we were to contemplate jumping off a cliff or walking into heavy, speeding traffic. We are talking about tormenting fear. That fear is of the devil.

> *It had been 30 years since I had a single fear, anxiety, or panic attack. Yes, the last attack I had was when I was 20 and now I am 50. I had a series of panic attacks and my mind was FRETTING and DESPAIRING. I could feel physical damage was being done in my liver and my heart. These lasted six months, with maybe one per week. This is how I put a stop to it: First, I cried out to the Lord my God and He delivered me from my fears. The way he did this was He told me four words. Yes, he gave me four words. I spoke the words into the air and they landed on my ears and my spiritual ears as well. When my own spirit man inside me heard these words, he brought instant relief. HERE are the four words: "Only Good Awaits Me." The peace that came was immediate, powerful, and so very peaceful.*

> *Next, to heal from the physical damage, I was told that a merry heart with gladness works as medicine. So, the entire weekend, I made sure I was smiling and made sure to have a happy heart full of gratefulness and gladness. I sang songs in church and through the day. I could experience healing going on inside of me. I had gotten together with a dear friend and we prayed for my total healing. YOU need to know that a major help to this is being well rested . . . as in getting plenty of sleep by going to bed on time!!! or even one hour earlier than usual. Not getting enough sleep is sure enough cause of the FEARSOME TRIGGER by itself. Later that month, as I was talking with God, He told me that what had happened is I had fallen into the proverbial "Pit of Despair." That is the actual name of it. Sometimes our minds get balled up . . . and wrapped around the axle . . . and you MUST KNOW THE DRILL . . . Here's the DRILL: "This man cried out to the Lord and He delivered me out of my fears." You cry out to God and He delivers you. You cry out to God and He delivers you. You cry out to God and He delivers you. You cry out to God and He delivers you. He is Faithful. Sometimes . . . you just need God. I have not had any more panic or anxiety attacks. (Man of God)*

"There are two basic motivating forces: fear and love. When we are afraid, we pull back from life. When we are in love, we open to all that life has to offer with passion, excitement, and acceptance. We need to learn to love ourselves first, in all our glory and our imperfections. If we cannot love ourselves, we cannot fully open to our ability to love others or our potential to create. Evolution and all hopes for a better world rest in the fearlessness and open-hearted vision of people who embrace life."

—John Lennon

**Life Reflections**

Pray that:

- The chain of fear and anxiety is broken over your life

- God will show areas of self-centeredness in your life

- God will make all things beautiful in your life

- God will teach you how to live in His finished word

Consider:

1. What causes you to be fearful?

2. How do you plan to overcome the cause?

# CHAPTER 5

# Brought Low to High

G od delivered John Johns (real person, fictitious name) from low self-esteem and a lack of self-worth that had led to an addiction to prostitutes, pornography, and illicit sex. In John's words, people often look at children who get into trouble and they wonder how they could do such a thing. We think they are supposed to be perfect children. They come from a family with two professional parents, live in a big home in the suburbs, attend the best school, and have a fancy car. For most children, the pain or insecurities that cause them to act out (in whatever way they do) began developing much earlier. Most of our families and friends love us and they see nothing but good things about us. Little do they know, feelings of self-doubt are growing within us. In America, we too often measure happiness by how much money and material possessions we have or how beautiful or handsome a person is. Kids discover something adults don't know, have forgotten, or do not care to think about. They know that money and looks are not the keys to happiness. Longing for ultimate happiness, they cry out for help. If kids do not receive adequate love, they will go searching for happiness in wrong places. John tells all:

*I do not come from a well-to-do family, but like those children, the self-doubt and lack of self-worth started growing in me at an early age. Because I stayed in school, got good grades, stayed in church, and took care of my sick mother, I appeared to be a perfect child and nobody knew the inner conflict. My mother started having nervous breakdowns when I was ten years old. My father was shot and killed when my mother was two months pregnant with me. She already had five kids before me, and she had another child after me. The pressure from raising seven children by herself and losing her home caused the nervous breakdowns.*

*Because of my mother's illness, my siblings turned to drugs to deal with the pain. Told I was the smartest, I was obligated to care for my mother and try to keep the family together. Before this happened, I was very shy and quiet. I had no confidence and very low self-esteem. Even though I made the grade at school, I could not get to first base on a personal level. Thus, once I became everybody's hero and the one everybody looks up to, I withdrew inward. I became a recluse, spent so much time being an adult in a child's body that I lost the ability to relate to people my own age, and could not communicate with girls.*

*One night in April 1984, I was walking home. I was 16-years-old and a virgin. I saw a prostitute standing on a corner. The devil told me, "You better get her because that is the only way you will ever get a woman." I agreed with him and I believed that lie for the next 13-1/2 years. I paid prostitutes to have sex with me. These women did not need me to talk, open up, or share. Whenever I met a girl who was bold enough to make the first move, I assumed the real me would turn her off. It was easier for me to pay a prostitute and not have to face possible rejection. Thus, I could continue to hide and not attack these issues. When people first get into the world of pornography and illicit sex, the devil can make it so exciting. You get to experiment with many kinds of people. You can fulfill any fantasy because if one person did not, the other would. The only question for me was whether I had the money to pay. When a sexual encounter with one woman was no longer satisfying, I turned to couples. These wives and girlfriends were beautiful, decent, clean, respectable, and intelligent and I did not have to pay. Such experiences made me worse, not better.*

*The devil does not tell the consequences of this behavior. This lifestyle damaged my emotions, my whole perspective on life, and my ability to give myself to one person. Even women who choose to do it for themselves and not for a pimp or boyfriend are impacted. They reach a point in which they are sick and tired of this lifestyle but they feel trapped. I got to the point in which I thought I was nothing. I felt lower than the dirt that people walk on every day. That was how I treated myself and that was how I expected others to treat me.*

*Arrested for the first time in June 1994 in one of the red light districts in San Francisco, I got off easy taking part in pretrial diversion to get the charges dismissed. In December 1996, I was arrested again in another red light district. This time, I had to hire a lawyer to fight for me. At first, I still did not see the need to change. During the months of plea-bargaining, the Lord got my attention and told me this is the last time I will get off easy. The charges were reduced to breach of the peace and had pretrial diversion again and counseling. I did not want to be saved, but I knew the Lord was calling me and I was miserable. April 1997 I stood up in front of the whole congregation, repented, and was baptized in Jesus's Name. I did not commit myself. I did not allow God to fill me with His Spirit (the*

*Holy Ghost). I had nothing to fight the devil with when he came back to tempt me to pick up prostitutes again.*

*Part of my plea bargain agreement required me to take counseling. A counselor started his job the same week I started attending the group counseling sessions. This counselor had the same problem I had when he was younger. He treated my problem from a carnal-minded point of view. He thought I needed to have one good experience with a decent woman who liked me for who I am. His talks helped me to recognize that I did have a problem. At the same time, I knew that his advice was not reaching deep enough. A friend at work offered to introduce me to a friend of his girlfriend. I knew right away that this relationship was not right, but I was excited by the opportunity to date someone the normal way. The relationship was a disaster because I still had unresolved issues. The failed relationship pushed me back to the streets.*

*On November 20, 1997, it happened again, arrested for solicitation. When I saw the police lights flashing this time, the only thing I could say was, "Oh God, you warned me." I knew I could not run anymore because God kept running me into brick walls. I spent the next three weeks trying to get myself in the mindset to give my life to Christ because I knew that He was the one who could break me from this terrible habit. On December 14, 1997, I was baptized again. Once Christ came into my life, I had the power to resist the temptations of the devil. I have found what I and everyone else longs for: Ultimate happiness, inner peace, and freedom. God has shown me who I am and what my purpose in life is. He has taught me how to love myself, how to respect myself, how to take care of myself, how to treat a woman, and how to give myself to my future wife.*

*From the moment Christ came into my life, I knew I was delivered and I felt a need to go back to the red light districts and let people know that there is hope because I found the answer. In March 1999, God called me to the Ministry and told me to do just that. In May 1999, I got the courage to walk the same streets that I used to go to pick up women. I talk to women I used to know, women I have never met, pimps, drug addicts, drug dealers, and anyone else who will listen. Then I explain to them how God has changed my life. I feed them if they are hungry and provide shelter. They are so afraid of leaving the abusive relationships because they are afraid that they will be alone and not have anyone to love them. It is my job to be a living example for them; to show them that they can be happy with Jesus alone. Even though God is powerful enough to save anyone in an instant, it does not happen that way. There is a cleansing that a person has to go through. Oftentimes when a person is suffering, that person can internalize that he/she is the only one in the world who is feeling this pain. If someone had, come to me when I was still sleeping around, that conversation would have started me to thinking about getting my life together.*

Low self-esteem and self-worth are prevalent among singles because we have no one in the physical to affirm us. Even people with exceptional talents are insecure and struggle with low or unhealthy self-esteem. Most people have low self-esteem and insecurities because of what someone projected on them. Self-esteem is your overall opinion of yourself—how you view your abilities and limitations. If you tend to focus more on your weaknesses or flaws than your positive qualities, you have esteem issues. If you receive negative feedback and take on rejection, you are likely to have esteem issues. Healthy esteem is recognizing your flaws and still having a good opinion of yourself and abilities. When you know your worth, you invite the respect of others without demand. God says, "You are altogether beautiful, my love, there is no flaw in you" (Song of Sol. 4:7, ESV). Other signs of low self-esteem are passiveness, indecisiveness, difficulty establishing healthy relationships, addiction, anxiety, inability to accept compliments, controlling spirit, fear of failure, and so on. It can come from abuse as a child, excessive criticism, comparison to others, unrealistic life expectations, peer pressure, financial or social position, betrayal, or other negative experiences.

With regard to self-image, adults struggle with many of the same issues that adolescents do. Adulthood is full of opportunities, challenges, and experiences that affect this. Everyone should be aware of how it can affect different areas of their life and relationships with others. Self-esteem is a very complicated matter, but I will try to simplify it. People who feel they are awkward can be divided into two categories. The first are people who had more or less stable, supportive home lives growing up but lack self-confidence because they were never that successful when it came to socializing. The second types are not doing well with other people, which hampers their self-confidence. Their lack of self-esteem goes much deeper because they did not have happy childhoods. They grew up in unhealthy environments and possibly experienced abuse or trauma. Even if they solved their social issues tomorrow, they would still have deep-seated issues with their self-worth.

*"But you are a chosen race, a royal priesthood, a dedicated nation [God's] own purchased, special people, that you may set forth the wonderful deeds, and display the virtues and perfections of Him who called you out of the darkness into His marvelous light"* (1 Pet 2:9, AMP)

You may not realize how important self-respect is. Your career, relation-ships, and your overall happiness depend on the level of confidence you have in yourself. If you do not believe that you have what it takes to succeed, you will not succeed. That promotion, raise, or new business opportunity will stay a distant dream until you develop the boldness and the drive to pursue it. Self-confidence makes the difference between an unhappy desk clerk and the CEO of the compa-ny. Dissatisfaction in relationships can be a result of low self-esteem as well. Neg-ative thoughts about "who you are" hinder creativity, rob you of simple joy, and stop you from seeing your own potential for greatness. No matter how good things around you may be, complete wholeness and happiness cannot come unless you have a healthy, positive image of yourself. Put yourself in the other person's shoes. People who do not love themselves are very difficult to love. Having re-spect for yourself and confidence enough to know that you are worthy of anoth-er's love can improve your relationship. Having children makes it even more crucial to have healthy self-regard. Young children can develop habits of negative commentary by watching you. Your children will learn from your example and their image of themselves depends on how you treat yourself and them. Friends, family, and colleagues are affected by your self-worth, too. It is harmful, but peo-ple with poor self-images put others down to make themselves feel better. Even if this does not happen, your low confidence can push people away. It is hard to be around someone who is negative toward themselves.

We are three-dimensional people with three views: the view of God in us, the opinions others hold about us, and our perception of ourselves. When you are insecure, you have low self-esteem or lack of assurance. Insecurities and low self-esteem leave you vulnerable and open for attack. "And, behold, there was a wom-an which had a spirit of infirmity eighteen years, and was bowed together, and could in no wise lift up herself. And when Jesus saw her, He called her to Him, and said unto her, Woman, thou art loosed from thine infirmity" (Luke 13:11-12, KJV). In Greek, infirmity (astheneia) means, "want of strength." Notice the scrip-ture says she had a "spirit of infirmity," not just that she "had an infirmity."

Could it be that this woman's physical ailment was a direct result of an emotional or spiritual battle? Emotional wounds, if not treated, can affect you physically. Notice Jesus said, "Woman, thou art (present tense) loosed (past tense) from thine infirmity." This woman was healed and set free from the condition that kept her looking down. You may have allowed your "spirit of infirmity," spe-cifically called low self-esteem, keep you from looking up to what is set in order.

Isaiah 53:5 says Jesus was wounded for our transgressions and with His stripes, we are (presently) healed (past tense). Low self-esteem weakens us. When we carry ourselves in a bowed-downed state, we are not looking up to the hills from whence our help comes. When we are in our bowed state of mind, we hurt ourselves—weight issues, feelings of inadequacy, and feeling unattractive are symptoms of emotional or spiritual problems. Once you discover the root, the origin of your low self-esteem, then administer God's prescribed Word.

T. D. Jakes said, "Although the problem may be rooted in the past, the prescription is a present word from God . . . the word you are hearing today is able to heal your yesterday!"

This woman carried her infirmity 18 years; yours may be twice as long. It is time for you to lift up and look up. Are you listening to the command, "_____, thou art loosed"?

> EVERY TIME YOU FOCUS ON YOUR FLAWS AND SHORT-COMINGS, YOU ARE DENYING THAT YOU ARE FEARFULLY AND WONDERFULLY MADE.

To break out, first you must see yourself as God sees you. "Oh yes, You shaped me first inside, then out; You formed me in my mother's womb. I thank you, High God—You're breathtaking! Body and soul, I am marvelously made! I worship in adoration—what a creation! You know me inside and out, You know every bone in my body; You know how I was made, bit by bit, how I was sculpted from nothing into something. As an open book, You watched me grow from conception to birth; the stages of my life were spread out before you, the days of my life prepared before I'd even lived one day" (Ps. 139:13-16, MSG). Develop a biblical view of yourself. Every time you focus on your flaws and shortcomings, you are denying that you are fearfully and wonderfully made. Second, you must change how you feel emotionally about yourself. Esteem is based on emotions, not self-image. You will have to adjust two things in your core beliefs: 1) that you are not good enough, and 2) the success you feel you should be. Lastly, you should work on developing your strengths. Find ways to create small victories, and then build from there. Low self-esteem is not your fault, inherent flaw, or disability. Your surroundings influenced you to create such factors. But you must believe that you have the power to be what is within.

Try on the following self-esteem exercises for size. The purpose of these exercises is to get you in the habit of expressing praise toward yourself. Each day, the goal is to record at least one thing you did right. If you don't have a particular event to write down, fill in the blanks of the following types of sentences:

- The thing I do best is _____.
- Something I have accomplished is _____.
- One of my best character traits is _____.
- I am proud of myself for _____.
- I am working to improve _____.

Give yourself time for meditation and reflection. In this quiet time, picture your-self succeeding at the activity that causes you self-doubt. Picture yourself as a suc-cessful public speaker, for example, or handling yourself at ease in a social setting. Self-esteem exercises can include affirmations. Make positive statements to your-self first thing in the morning, before the concerns of the day have set in. Several times a day, continue to repeat such statements:

- I am confident in my ability to handle whatever will come up today.
- I am improving every day.
- I deserve to be happy and successful.

Another technique I use in leadership coaching self-esteem is to answers the question, "How do I feel about who I am?" We learn self-esteem in our family of origin; we do not inherit it.

- **Identify triggers to low self-esteem.** We personalize stressful events
  (e.g., criticism) by inferring a negative meaning about ourselves. A self-defeating action often follows. Instead, each event can be a chance to learn about ourselves—if we face our fear of doing so and the negative beliefs about ourselves that sustain the negative meanings.

  1.

  2.

  3.

- **Acknowledge reaction.** Verbalize, "Here I go again (describe the action, feeling, thought) . . ." Actively do something with the awareness, rather than passively note it. The result is to slow the impulse and give ourselves a choice about how we want to respond.

- **Choose response.** Hold self-defeating impulses. Instead, act in a self-caring and effective way. By choosing to act in a more functional way, we take a step toward facing our fears.

    1.

    2.

    3.

- **Positive Affirmation Statements.**

    1.

- **Develop skills.** We can give for our own safety, engender hope, tolerate confusion, and raise self-esteem by learning and using these essential life skills:

    o **Experience feelings.** "Feel" feelings in your body and name your needs. When we do not respect our feelings, we are left to rely on what others want and believe.

    o **Optional thinking.** End "either/or" thinking. Think in "shades of gray" and learn to reframe meanings. By giving ourselves options, we open ourselves to new possibilities about how to think about our dilemmas.

    o **Detachment.** End all abuse; say "no" to misrepresentations and assumptions. By maintaining personal boundaries, we discourage abuse by others and assert our separateness.

- o **Assertion.** Voice what you see, feel, and want by making "I" statements. By expressing our thoughts, feelings, and desires in a direct and honest manner, we show that we are in charge of our lives.

- o **Receptivity.** End self-absorption; listen to others' words and meanings to restate them. In this way, we act with awareness of our contribution to events as well as empathize with the needs of others.

"I have told you these things, so that in Me you may have [perfect] peace *and* confidence. In the world you have tribulation *and* trials *and* distress *and* frustration; but be of good cheer [take courage; be confident, certain, undaunted]! For I have overcome the world. [I have deprived it of power to harm you and have conquered it for you]" (John 6:33, AMP). The Christian life is an overcoming life. Through Jesus, we are able to overcome every personal struggle and problem. Because of Him, we have victory over the world, including low self-esteem. Everyone has feelings of inferiority, condemnation, and hopelessness from time to time. Since the Garden of Eden, Satan has used lies to destroy people and take them further from the truth of God's word. Satan will accuse you and do everything in his power to make you feel defeated, including playing with your self-esteem. This is why you must stand firm on the promises of God and see yourself as valuable in the Kingdom and to God.

---

"Self-esteem is the switch in the circuit of your life that dims or brightens your future. Bring it low and you don't shine your light; raise it up and you brighten the corner where you are."

—Israelmore Ayivor

## Life Reflections

Pray for:

- Strength, patience, and longsuffering

- A renewed mind

- Healing of low-self esteem

Consider:

1. Have you had experiences with low self-esteem?

2. What are some of the accusations that Satan made against you?

3. How has God assured you of your worth and His love?

4. Why do you think it is important for your self-esteem to respond to criticism with love and forgiveness?

# CHAPTER 6

# Building Blocks

An old hymn says that life is filled with swift transitions. Every day you are charged with making decisions and choices. When all cylinders are clicking, decisions and choices will line up with God's vision for us and the goals we set. We have distractions pulling us away from the intended mark. The technician who services my heating and cooling is fascinated with race cars, thus he always tells me an encouraging race car story. He once told me about a race car driver pushing his car across the finish line claiming first place in the race. This driver never stopped at the pit stops, which gave him a huge lead. Therefore, when he ran out of gas, he was able to push his way across the finish line. The moral of the story is many of us are stopping at pit stops God wants us to pass. Sometimes the push is enough to get you through the life experiences. The other point is that we are staying at the pit stops too long. Using pit stops is not a bad thing, but your pit stops are brief life lessons God uses to prepare you to cross the finish line. Staying too long will delay the plans God has for your life. Staying too long will provoke you to make decisions and choices based on temporal things. If the race car driver had stopped at every pit stop, he would have had to work harder and longer to reach his intended goal.

As we transition through life, there will be pit stops on every journey. Some are designed to build you and others to distract you. This is why Paul taught us, "But I say walk *and* live [habitually] in the [Holy] Spirit [responsive to *and* controlled *and* guided by the Spirit]; then you will certainly not gratify the cravings *and* desires of the flesh (of human nature without God)" (Gal. 5:16, AMP). Every choice and decision you make in life will have pros and cons. Each one will pull you or push you; will bring joy and peace or confusion. Discipleship is key to

*As we transition through life, there will be pit stops on every journey. Some are designed to build you and others to distract you.*

making sure you are always advancing in life and crossing the finish line, not hanging out at the pit stops. Without discipleship, you will always be toying with life choices that pull you away and cause confusion.

"Then Jesus said to His disciples, If anyone desires to be My disciple, let him deny himself [disregard, lose sight of, and forget himself and his own interests] and take up his cross and follow Me [cleave steadfastly to Me, conform wholly to My example in living, and if need be, in dying, also]" (Matt 16:24, AMP). A disciple is a learner, student, and imitator of Jesus Christ. Disciples reflect the opinion, value system, and perspective of the Master. They submit their desires, opinions, and perspectives for that of their Lord and Savior Jesus Christ—so much so that they can be identified by their lifestyle according to the Master's lifestyle. Their speech and actions resemble that of disciples. To be a disciple requires submission. When people see a disciple, they see Jesus because the disciple is associated and affiliated. You can be a friend from afar; Jesus is not just looking for friends. He is looking for followers because you can be a friend and not *know* the person; you can just know *of* them. To be a follower requires a personal relationship and connection. Jesus is in control and has authority to rule on a disciple's behalf. In Matthew 28, when Jesus talks about delegating authority, He is talking to those disciples who are submitted and imitate Him. In most of our lives, we have an authority issue. Police officers are delegated authority by the governmental system in which they work. If you attack an officer, you are attacking the entire system they represent. It is the same way in the Kingdom: When the enemy comes against you, he is coming against He whom you represent. Jesus delegated authority to you, but He still has all authority and He will act on your behalf if you are a disciple.

Many profess Christianity, but not many are submitted to the Lordship of Jesus Christ. Those who are submitted are recognized as disciples and are delegated authority. You can be saved, content with going to heaven, and yet not make an impact while living on earth. In your singleness, realities, troubles, weaknesses, and strengths, God desires to get glory out of your life. God is not concerned with your church membership; He is concerned with you being a disciple so you can disciple. Until you are submitted to the Lordship over your life, you are professing to be a Christian but not living out your faith. When you give your life to Jesus Christ, you no longer belong to the world. You are reclassified and now belong to the community of God. Discipleship is not a choice; it is mandatory. Is your story any different than these?

Female, Age Range: 31-40

*My story is not extravagant, riddled with hardship, or dramatic book material, but amazing. My God saw fit to give me loving, God-fearing parents and surround me with a community of believers. I asked God into my heart when I was five years old. I was watching TV when I decided to ask my mom about salvation, and told her that I wanted to be a part of it. She prayed with me and started crying, though she swore to me she wasn't crying. I believe that I was saved that afternoon, but my life didn't change until a little later.*

*I grew up in the church, and was there every time the doors were open—be it Saturday cleanings, Sunday mornings, or Wednesday youth activities. I knew all the answers and could recite my catechism without stumbling. The thing that I lacked was heart knowledge. Until about 5th or 6th grade, I was using my salvation as a "get out of Hell free" card, but when I hit middle school this began to change. I became a huddle leader for my school's FCA program and in doing so, along with the challenges from my outstanding Sunday school teacher, I began to grow in my relationship with Christ and allowed His love to change my life.*

*Since that time in my life, I have enjoyed getting to know my God and glorifying Him with my life. I am involved and am being discipled by one of the leaders in our ministry. This has been monumental in my walk with Christ. I have someone praying for me, talking with me, laughing with me, crying with me, and challenging me daily to walk closer and more intimately with my Savior. Am I perfect? Not even close, but I know that one day I will be, and I will get to spend eternity in a party celebrating my God.*

Male, Age Range: 31-40

*In my youth, I was discipled by a man of GOD. Since then, I have in turn discipled others in the ways of the LORD and into a deeper understanding of HIS word. The following has proven to be a good description of my life since coming to GOD. I have, over the last several weeks, seen mankind in their most natural and elemental existence—the disorder and the destructive life styles, the consequences of following other gods. Just like the many examples we find in the scriptures, the natural man cannot know GOD without the HOLY SPIRIT to draw and instruct him; just like a blind person can't enjoy the beauty of a sunset or sunrise, or the deaf person a sound lyric. I cannot understand nor do I wish to return to this lifestyle. The quandary that I have is following GOD even when HE leads us into darkness through relationships that are destructive and chaotic. How is it that people live this lifestyle and are content to wallow in it? I understand better why Jonah ran from*

*GOD's directive to go to Nineveh; we all know how that ended for Jonah. To be sure of GOD's call and direction, we must trust in the holy writings and what we have learned along the way. There is no running from GOD.*

> But you have faithfully followed my teaching, way of life, purpose, faith, patience, love, endurance, persecutions, and sufferings that happened to me in Antioch, in Iconium, and in Lystra, what persecutions I endured, and the Lord delivered me from all of them. And indeed, all those who want to live in a godly manner in Christ Jesus will be persecuted. But evil people and imposters will progress to the worse, deceiving and being deceived. But you continue in the things which you have learned and are convinced of, because you know from whom you learned them, and that from childhood you have known the holy writings that are able to make you wise for salvation through faith in Christ Jesus. All scripture is inspired by God and profitable for teaching, for reproof, for correction, for training in righteousness, in order that the person of God may be competent, equipped for every good work. (2 Tim. 3:10–17, LEB)

Before you can start building you in the natural, you must start with the spiritual. Single and married alike understand the concept of growth in the physical development of humans and know its importance. Growth is just not for new believers, but also for those who have been walking with Christ for time. Perhaps you have not been the disciple you should have been, or you have operated in strife because of ignorance, or have met an obstacle because of irregular attendance at church, worldliness, or indifference. Whatever your issue may be, you can decide today to grow toward maturity. Just as a baby needs to do certain things to grow, so Christians need certain kinds of activities to grow. Taken from Gospel Way Ministries (www.gospelway.com), growth hinges on:

## A DESIRE TO GROW

<u>You Will Never Grow unless You Want to Grow.</u>

In the physical realm, children want to grow. "I want to grow up to be just like Mommy/Daddy/Michael Jordan . . . " or, "I can't wait 'till I'm 16 so I can drive." Parents and kids become so excited when kids learn something new—their first step, first word, first drawing, and so forth. Everyone wants children to develop new abilities. Parents sometimes use this to encourage children. Likewise, in spiritual matters, Christians must want to grow. Desire the pure milk of the word that you may grow thereby (1 Pet. 2:2). Some seem to like being spiritual babies. They do not want to grow. It is easy to be a baby—no responsibility. Others feed you, clothe you, and change your diaper. In the church, you do not have to teach, rebuke sin, or do work. It is a free ride! However, being a baby is not the goal of life. We are born babies so we can grow and become productive and useful. Likewise, we are born again, so we can become mature Christians, serving the Lord. One of the conditions for becoming a child of God is repentance. One must decide to turn from sin and go to work in God's vineyard. Then one must bring forth the fruits of repentance. This will lead us to grow and improve in God's work. Otherwise, we have not accomplished our purpose for becoming children of God. Jesus set an example for us, and we should follow in His steps (1 Pet. 2:21). We should ask ourselves, "Do I want to grow up to be spiritually strong like Jesus?"

<u>You Must Maintain this Desire to Grow.</u>

Members who once wanted to grow may lose that want. They may start on fire for the Lord but lose their zeal. They develop a spirit of indifference or negligence. Others develop a level of maturity and stagnate. They are satisfied, thinking no more growth is needed. The Scriptures teach that growth is always needed. Even Paul, as mature as he was, did not consider himself to have achieved perfection (maturity) such that he could cease striving to improve (Phil. 3:12-14). He forgot achievements (and failures) and pressed on to greater accomplishments. Peter thought he had reached a level where he would never deny Jesus. But that very night he denied Him three times (Matt. 26:31-35). Therefore, let him who thinks he stands take heed lest he fall (1 Cor. 10:12). Christians never reach the point of being so mature that we cannot fall. One of the main reasons Christians do not grow is that they do not see the need for growing. They have no desire to work and serve to their full ability. When people develop a burning hunger and thirst to work for the Lord, they will develop the other steps they need to grow.

Do you have that burning desire to do more for the Lord? Have you set specific goals of work you want to do for God, improvements to make, new levels to reach?

## NOURISHMENT

<u>You Need Spiritual Food from God's Word.</u>

A child cannot grow without proper food. Good parents are concerned about proper nutrition. They want children to eat what is good, not bad, for them. Pictures of children starving in poverty touch us. Most children want nourishment. Babies cry for food. Once, as a child, I got so hungry I cried, and my mother felt bad. Even adults know we need food and do not like to go long without it. We want it every day, several times a day. Likewise, we cannot grow without feeding on God's Word. Grow in the grace and knowledge of our Lord and Savior Jesus Christ (2 Pet. 3:18). Man shall not live by bread alone but by every word that proceeds from the mouth of God (Eph. 4:15; Matt. 4:4; Matt. 5:6).

<u>To Get this Nourishment, We Must Study the Bible and Attend Church Services.</u>

Scriptures show the need for regular nourishment. Christians were rebuked for not growing as they should have, because they had not studied (Heb. 5:11-14). Repeatedly, members fall away or are spiritual midgets because they do not eat properly. Bereans were able to know truth because they searched the Scriptures daily (Acts 17:11). We need regular nourishment. Meditate on God's word day and night (Ps. 1:1-2). Children and adults need physical food, and get very upset without it. But, are we content to go for days at a time without feeding on God's word? (Ps. 119:47-48, 95-99; Josh. 1:8).

Do we make use of the opportunities the church provides for nourishment? I never cease to be amazed when the church provides a spiritual feast, and members choose to do other things. How often do we miss the regular meals provided for our bellies?

Take this test to check your spiritual nourishment. How much time did you spend this week watching TV? How much time watching sports or entertainment? Or spent reading the paper, magazines, and so on? How much time did you spend on hobbies or outside interest that may not be immoral, but are not necessary? How many hours did you spend studying your Bible? How many services of the church did you attend? How many did you miss that you could have attended? Which do you nourish the best: your spirit or your body? Are you feeding your mind on God's word or on pleasures? Christians need regular nourishment from God's word to grow.

## EXERCISE AND PRACTICE

### Exercise and Practice Are Essential to Physical Development.

Athletes and musicians know they must exercise and practice to improve. Developing skills requires continual repetition: playing a song, throwing pitches, shooting baskets. Athletes run, lift weights, and practice hour after hour to grow strong and develop endurance. Illustration: A man once had an apartment next to a professional cello player. He thought it must be exciting to play in an orchestra—until he listened as the cellist practiced the scales, exercises, and songs endlessly.

Children practice skills repeatedly to learn them. Children learning to walk try again and again. They are proud to learn a new word, and then they use it until they drive you crazy! They want to play the same thing repeatedly: play the same tape recording, put the same clothes on the same doll. Parents encourage children to repeat what they must learn: they drill math facts, spelling, reading, and piano. They get tired, but we encourage them because that is how they learn. "Practice makes perfect"—or at least it promotes improvement.

### Exercise and Practice Are Essential to Spiritual Growth.

Those who are of full age, because of use have their senses exercised to discern both good and evil (Heb. 5:14). Growth requires exercise as well as nourishment. Exercise yourself toward godliness (1 Tim. 4:7). Like children, athletes, and musicians, we must work again and again at applying Bible principles to become effective in the Lord's work.

Applications: To learn to teach, we must do it repeatedly; teach your children, teach home studies and Bible classes, preach sermons—again and again. To learn to lead singing, practice songs at home. Sing with your family, lead during church meetings—over and over again. To understand the Bible, study it repeatedly, talk to others, drill yourself, memorize. Get in and dig. To learn to pray, do it over and over again. Kids may not be good at activities at first, but parents encourage them to keep going. Likewise, older members must encourage newer ones to use their talents. They may not be skilled at first, but they learn by doing. We need to encourage teachers, preachers, and song leaders. Do not complain. Do not stay home. They need the practice!

## TIME AND PATIENCE

Do not Expect to Reach Your Goal Overnight.

Children do not become full-grown instantaneously. At birth, they are so small you can hold them in a little basket. Soon they are outgrowing new clothes every month. Eventually, they can wear their parents' clothes or even larger—but it takes time. Sometimes, children become impatient: "I can't wait 'till I'm 18 (or 21)." We say, "Take your time. It will come soon enough." Time passes and, sure enough, what they were waiting for has come and gone, and they are looking back wondering how the time passed so fast!

Likewise, do not expect maturity overnight. To become perfect and mature (entire), lacking nothing, we must have patience (James 1:4). Newborn Christians want to know everything and do everything right away. They may not be willing to take the time to study and develop ability. They want to be just like the mature members—and want other members to treat them with the same respect they do mature members—before they have taken time to grow. Sometimes, older members are impatient with new members. We do not understand why new converts have trouble with basic concepts. Then sometimes these new members explain, "I never was taught the Bible." They have no background in the Scriptures, and it takes time to grow. Remember that people who may be mature today did not get that way overnight. It took years of study and practice. Moreover, new converts will not become mature overnight. It will take time. New members should not get discouraged and give up. Older members should not be impatient or demanding. Remember how our children took time to grow, and how we had to show patience with their immature ways as they grew. But growth will come, as long as people are trying and we give them time.

<u>Do not Become Discouraged by Mistakes and Rebukes.</u>

Children make many mistakes and often must be told they are wrong. How often does a child fall while learning to walk? They fall again and again, gathering bumps and bruises. They spill their milk, do not hold their spoon, fall off their bikes, and come to bat in the bottom of the ninth with the winning run in scoring position, and strike out. Parents correct, instruct, and punish until we almost feel sorry for the kids. Growing up is tough! If kids are going to become mature, they have to keep going in spite of mistakes and rebukes. And someday, they will look back on their own childish mistakes and just smile.

Likewise, new converts will make many mistakes and often must be told they are wrong. The greatest Bible characters committed terrible errors and had to be rebuked:

- Moses made excuses when God called him to lead Israel out of bondage.
- David committed adultery with Bathsheba and was rebuked by Nathan.
- Peter denied Jesus three times.
- Paul persecuted Christians before his conversion.
- Thomas doubted Jesus's resurrection.
- All the apostles forsook Jesus when He was arrested and crucified.

Shortly after he had confessed Jesus and praised (Matt. 16:21-23; 15-18), Peter contradicted Jesus and was rebuked. Yet all of these are remembered as some of God's greatest servants. Great servants are not those who live without ever sinning, but people who learn from their mistakes and go on to serve God faithfully. Judas betrayed Jesus and is remembered as a traitor. Peter denied Jesus three times and is remembered as a great Apostle. What is the difference? Judas, after betraying Jesus, hung himself. Peter, after denying Jesus, repented and went to work preaching the gospel. A person is destroyed, not because he errs, but because he becomes stubborn when he is rebuked and will not repent (Prov. 29:1). What is needed is repentance and patience to learn to do right.

The story is told of a little boy who fell out of bed. Asked what happened, he said, "I guess I just stayed too close to the getting'-in place." That is why many people fall away from God after their conversion—they stay too close to the "getting'-in" place and do not grow to maturity. It is no shame to be a baby, if you were born a few months ago. But, a person who has been a child of God for several years and has not grown has a problem. Everyone needs to grow as a Christian, and everyone can grow, if they apply the Bible principles of growth. Can you identify with this man?

*I am 76 years old and God wants me to take another giant step before it is too late! There is another aspect to moving forward in Christian growth, and that is to realize that the devil wants to kick us around. We know we are forgiven, yet feelings of guilt, inferiority, and shame threaten to overwhelm us. That is nothing but a lie from the devil, so we must stand up and trample him underfoot! Romans 8:1 (NKJV) says, "There is therefore now no condemnation to those who are in Christ Jesus, who do not walk according to the flesh, but according to the Spirit." Also, reading Romans 8:14-26 will give you encouragement. After growing up in a Christian home and being baptized as a teenager, I drifted for 30 years. I had a vague feeling that all was not well, but did not realize how far I had fallen. With considerable difficulty, I did hold onto a job but was not getting ahead. I had lost rapport with my family (wife and three children), felt lonely, and even bitter at times. I even looked at horoscopes, but found that evil spirits were starting to cater to me. I prayed that God would show me how to straighten out my life. Then God gave me a dream in which I was on my way to hell, and I knew why. That shook me up! For the next seven days, upon returning home from work, I knelt by my bed and wept for Jesus to wash me clean. Then I felt refreshed! I asked God what the next step would be, upon which a friend invited me to a Full Gospel Businessmen's meeting. What a thrill. I have never been the same since! I would let go of God, but in His mercy, He had not let go of me. In His love, He drew me closer to Himself than I had ever been before. My wife and I took part in a Bible study for couples, which helped us to find one another again. God is now leading me day by day to serve Him. There is so much to do and so little time. Yet with His guidance, people are helped and I am blessed. Please do not get the impression that I have got it made. The journey continues, and the devil must again be trampled underfoot. Spiritual growth is a continuous process! See you at Jesus's Banqueting Table.*

By definition, growth requires time. It is progress and development as time passes. Three things in this world you cannot fix quickly: growing spiritually, losing weight, and building wealth. As demonstrated in this chapter, growth is a process. But, if you check the consumer reports, these are billion-dollar industries. I cannot tell you how many books and products I have purchased trying to find a shortcut around that which requires work. Naturally, we all will grow with little to no effort of our own. Spiritually, you have to put in the work to build yourself. Growing in your relationship with Jesus means to know Him better, to love Him, and to obey Him more. Just as it is natural for a child to grow in a loving relationship with a parent, it is natural for you to grow in your love relationship with God.

Four aspects of communication will help you develop your relationship with Jesus. God communicates with us through the Bible, revealing His character and His will. "All Scripture is inspired by God and is useful to teach us what is true and to make us realize what is wrong in our lives. It corrects us when we are wrong and teaches us to do what is right. God uses it to prepare and equip His people to do every good work" (2 Tim. 3:16-17, NLT). We communicate with God through prayer, sharing our thoughts, our needs, and our want to do His will. "Don't worry about anything; instead, pray about everything. Tell God what you need, and thank Him for all He has done. Then you will experience God's peace, which exceeds anything we can understand. His peace will guard your hearts and minds as you live in Christ Jesus" (Phil. 4:6-7, NLT). We communicate with Christians through fellowship, encouraging and building up one another. "Let us think of ways to motivate one another to acts of love and good works.

And let us not neglect our meeting together, as some people do, but encourage one another, now that the day of His return is drawing near" (Heb. 10:24-25, NLT). Spend time with other Christians to encourage each other to love and do well. The Greek word for fellowship, *koinonia*, means, "Sharing in common." We need to share our Christian experience with others who love God, and likewise allow them to share with us. God appoints the church as a place for us to meet other Christians and learn about God. Bible studies and other meetings are also helpful. We communicate with others who do not know God by sharing about our relationship with Jesus. "There is salvation in no one else! God has given no other name under heaven by which we must be saved" (Acts 4:12, NLT). Other suggestions are to set aside a time and place for daily personal Bible study and prayer. A good book to begin with is

*Naturally, we all will grow with little to no effort of our own. Spiritually, you have to put in the work to build yourself.*

the New Testament Book of John. As you read, underline verses you find meaningful. Pray and ask God to show you who He is and how you can respond to Him.

Now that you have accepted the charge and made the decision to mature, you can move in the direction of building in the natural. I now challenge you to build in the natural by making a list of areas you would like to improve in, and what you want to do. The next step is to come up with a plan or course of action. For example, you if you need to improve financially, take a financial class to learn how to be wise with your money. Accepting this challenge may require you to clean up your credit, get on a budget, pay off your debt, or go on a spending fast. For me it took all of these. In school, we were taught many things: how to write, how to count, how to spell words—but I do not remember a class on relationship communication. Learning how to communicate effectively is extremely important. It is something that we have to work on—for most of us, it does not come naturally. I suggest you read books, listen to podcasts, go to conferences—anything you can do to improve yourself on both sides of the communication process—better listening and better speaking. Needing to improve communication skills is common among singles. It takes constant engagement of interaction.

Not giving attention to needy areas is like the foolish man building his house on sand. Your foundation will be faulty at best, and everything that you do in the natural will not last or bring joy. Your spiritual foundation is prerequisite for all that you will do in life. Have you heard of the 80/20 (Pareto) principle? The 80/20 principle was suggested by Joseph Juran and named after the economist Vilfredo Pareto. Pareto realized that 20% of the Italian population was producing 80% of the income, thus indicating that the majority of outcomes were produced by a few causes. I was exposed to this principle years ago in a training class. Over the years since, I have come to discover the 80/20 principle can be applied to every area of my spiritual and natural life. It is important for you to understand that 20% of your activities account for 80% of your results in life. You spend 20% of your life pursuing your educational goals. Then 80% living the results of what you learned in school. Note that churches are supported by 20% of the membership. In the workplace, they say 20% of your time is doing what you planned and 80% is what others planned for you. If you take an inventory of your life, I am sure you will find a lot of 80/20 ratios.

From a different perspective, most Christians attend church two days per week—worship service and bible study. Those two days per week will produce the majority of your spiritual growth and affect your life the most. During times in my life, I wasted time doing activities I was not good at or did not like. I spent time procrastinating and not working efficiently. Like me, you probably spend 80% of your time producing things that do not add value to your life. In order to build you and become more fruitful in your season of singleness, you must hone in on that 20% and maximize the moment. There are things God wants you to perfect while waiting for your husband or wife. God uses His word to grow us up and train us. Anything that is contrary to the word of God is not His method of maturity. He is the one who is qualified to define you and He will show your immaturity. Others might point out areas of growth for you, but it is up to you and the Holy Spirit to frame your world.

"When I was ten, I read fairy tales in secret and would have been ashamed if I had been found doing so. Now that I am 50, I read them openly. When I became a man I put away childish things, including the fear of childishness and the desire to be very grown up."

—C. S. Lewis

**Life Reflections**

Pray for:

- Understanding and application of God's Word

- Wisdom in daily decisions

- A divine strategy for building the natural aspects of you

Consider:

1. How does God affect your decisions?

2. How does knowing God influence your actions and reactions?

# CHAPTER 7

# Barely R.E.A.L.

Sally (fictitious name) says: *I do not date and can count on one hand with fingers left over the number of relationships. Having a mean loner streak left me single for three years. My relationship with God never happened. When I had my confirmation at age 13, I stood up and left my peers at the front of the church while the entire congregation watched. It was not that I did not believe in God. I did. I just did not want to commit when I felt I had never met God in the church I had attended for my whole life. As I began dating, the normal insecurities ensued. I was damaged. In addition, without God to heal me, my bruised heart got broken in the next round. In addition, it happened repeatedly. My relationships never improved. "Single" me, in between relationships, was awful. I whined, was hung up on the past, and lost my passion for things outside my love life. I never learned and I never brought any wisdom to the table for the next relationship. My relationships were not so much commitment as an emotional addiction to give my insecurities a quick fix. Hearing a boyfriend tell me he loved me and that I was beautiful? How could I not become attached to it?*

*The last breakup hit me the hardest above the rest. I was giving God attention at the same time I had made a real commitment to that boyfriend. When our relationship fell apart, and this God I was, getting to know did not save it when I prayed for Him to, I was not a happy camper. My very young opinion of God made Him fall short in my eyes—and so I went to back to ignoring Him ... and hit a very cold rock bottom. Not only did I lose a man I was in love with, but also I lost friendships that for the first time I valued. I saw the emptiness of my job, and I got close and personal with a nice dose of depression. I was as single as single gets, which in my mind was synonymous with failure. But as much as I had committed to my boyfriend at the time, I had also committed to God. No matter how little of a space in your heart you have lent Him, He is taking that as a cue to do serious work in you. He did, through various signs in my life. But trust me, it was enough that I was listening now. This God, who sent a son to die for me knowing that I did not want Him anyway, still was not having my bull. He was not leaving, and He was not calling it quits. He was trying to win me over by showering me with gifts that I did not deserve.*

*This crazy desperation God had for me to love Him was disconcerting and even a little weird. I had never, ever had any boy want me like that. At that point, I was empty and very, very single. My non-memory foam bed had a very distinct outline of me because I never left it. I had no passion for my old hobbies, and with time to kill, I began to give it to God. And the more I focused on Him, the less I found myself thinking about my ex. The more God showed love to me, the more I began to find reasons why He would love me. The reasons I found were reasons I used to start loving myself. As I let God in (albeit slow), the more whole I felt. It was work, to be sure. For someone who does not commit, it was intense. I sought Him in others who had known Him for years, and I asked people about Him who knew nothing of Him. I read about Him. I talked to Him, instead of demanding things I wanted. I formed new passions. I felt a lot of guilt that someone I did not know died for me, for me to have wasted so much time trapped in a single state of mind. And just as sudden, a lot of love for Him followed, and I found myself committed.*

*Moreover, we flash forward to now. My life is in transition—it is moving forward, fast. My first paragraph still stands. I do not date, and rarely find myself feeling lonely. My lack of five-minute crushes, my lack of quick feelings, and the disappearance of my need for them worried me until I received a very clear insight as to why I no longer wanted to date around. For the first time, I am not waiting on a relationship to feed my insecurities. I am preparing for a relationship to fuel a hunger for God—a relationship with a man and God as the central line in it. One of the biggest things I have done in my commitment to God is to give Him my trust that He has a purpose for my life. If there is work to be done in and through me, I trust Him to give me a partner in crime for it or use my freedom and independence to make it happen. For now, it is through my independence. Now, I see "single" as an honor. It is a nod from God that you are enough to do His work just as you are. It is an opportunity to do work on your heart and to be better. To prepare yourself so you have so much to bring to the table when you meet your mate that he barely has room to put his elbows down. If I can leave you with one thing, there is absolutely no shame in being single.*

From my vantage point, one of the biggest issues within the single's community is that we tend to do everything others want us to do. We set our expectations based on what is going on around us. Like Sally (above), at some point we have to be R.E.A.L. with ourselves. Enough people often lie to themselves because the truth about their intent is hard to accept. Therefore, we let others dictate our timeframe for accomplishing our goals. We let others influence our mindset and thoughts. On a daily basis, others yield influence over our standards. If we do not decide to filter that influence, we are setting ourselves up to become puppets pulled by strings we cannot even see.

Increase your awareness and increase your personal power over your life. When you look in the mirror, you will like what you see more. The choice is yours: program yourself or be programmed by others. I am reminded of a song Michael Jackson released. He sings, "I'm starting with the man in the mirror—I'm asking him to change his ways—And no message could have been any clearer—If you want to make the world a better place, take a look at yourself and then make a change." The hardest person to fight against that you will ever meet may be the person who you imagine is looking at you from the other side of the mirror. We are our own worst critics, sizing ourselves up in ways that we would never judge other people, while resisting the acceptance of positive messages as "not a big deal." Many of us cannot stand to face the person staring at us in the bathroom mirror. Some even remove mirrors from their house because their self-loathing is so strong. This is all about looking at our self-image, our identity, the mishmash of opinions, feelings, and baggage we carry—and asking ourselves how it all comes together. The frightening thing is that for so many of us, our self-image is a prison; yet it's the single thing we have total control of in our lives. The morning mirror check can be a mini-accountability session that you experience every day, if you focus on who you want that person in the mirror to be. On the other hand, the mirror can be the scariest thing in the world if conditioned (whether by parental criticism, bad experience, or those beauty magazines) to look down on yourself. Before you change your ways, you must be R.E.A.L.. This is my acronym for Release, Examine, Account, and Live.

> We are our own worst critics, sizing ourselves up in ways that we would never judge other people, while resisting the acceptance of positive messages as "not a big deal."

### Release

"Forget about what's happened; don't keep going over old history. Be alert, be present. I'm about to do something brand-new. It's bursting out! Don't you see it? There it is! I'm making a road through the desert, rivers in the badlands" (Isa. 43:18-19, MSG).

You must be willing to let go of the past so you can live in the present and expect your future. Not just singles, but many people are bound by their past. Some have fallen prey to the lust of this world, others' opinions of them, having unrealistic expectations, strongholds, low esteem, and the list goes on and on. They are rehashing past disappointments, hurts, wounds, and discontentment. Singles, just like anyone else, are stuck having to deal with the realities of life. Feelings of being rejected, unforgiven, abandoned and low self-worth are running rampant. Everyone has issues that we must overcome as we live the victorious life. My issues stemmed from growing up without a father figure. Yours may come from not feeling loved as a child or being abused. Someone else's may come from not being affirmed, supported, or prepared for life. I'm sure there are those who feel their past was perfect, but the majority of men and women have suffered something in life that caused them to be stuck. If not in your upbringing, issues may have stemmed from situations you encountered as an adult. For example, your dream job snatched away; the person you thought you would marry married someone else; or your spouse left you. You may have lost your stability or your child delivered you news that shook your foundation. Whatever your past was, and in whatever way it changed you, recovery is in reach. You can push the restart button even in un-Christ-like situations. It doesn't matter whether you had a baby out of wedlock, lived with someone before marriage, had an abortion or paid for one, God loves you. I had to learn through my bad decision that no actions or circumstances can change God's plan for my life. Like you, I was holding myself hostage.

When I hear, "Let it go," "Get over it," "Move on," I recognize a need for healing. Even if a person lets go, the pain of the past remains. Such pain leads to bondage, broken hearts, emotional baggage, and unfruitfulness. Our past hurts live in our memories, which affects the way we think, make decisions, and experience life. I give to you four things you can do that will jumpstart letting go of yesterday's pain and embracing the promises of God today.

1. Quit rehashing the pain by talking about it. Instead, find an encouraging bible verse or short story to discuss. Every time you talk about the pain, you are waking it up and giving it control. This is why you get upset just thinking about it; before you know it, your entire mood has changed. Going forward, do not allow others to pull you into a conversation about past hurts.

2. Make a list of the past hurts, the emotions attached, and the names of those who caused the pain. This helps you release it from your spirit. For every hurt you write down, on a separate piece of paper write the life lesson you learned from it; also write down one thing you will pray for the

person who caused such hurt. This step allows you to release the offense associated with the hurt. Once you have the lesson written down and what you will pray for, you can trash or burn the list of hurts.

3. Repent for coming into agreement with every wound, thought, or emotion that has been controlling you. Call them out in prayer. True repentance is having a change of heart. What you thought was OK before, your conviction now tells you it is not. The difference between asking for forgiveness and repenting is you can ask for forgiveness and still practice a sinful lifestyle. You can ask for forgiveness and not have a change of heart, which is different from repenting. Once you repent, God does forgive you.

4. Break all agreements of bondage by confessing the word of God daily. Always remember that your soul is saturated with the blood of Jesus, you are filled with power, and your soul is excellent. I wrote my own personal faith confession that I spoke over my life every day for a period of time. If you made an agreement with feeling unforgiven; find or write a confession on such. The key is to make the confession at least daily. I promise each time you do this, you are diminishing the power that past hurt and pain once had over you.

The healthier your soul becomes, the easier it is to release your past pain. As you continue on this journey, you will learn to love, understand, and (re)act with God's word. Releasing the past, healing old hurts, and deliverance from emotional wounds will help you toward maturity.

Examine

"Test yourselves to make sure you are solid in the faith. Don't drift along taking everything for granted. Give yourselves regular checkups. You need firsthand evidence, not mere hearsay, that Jesus Christ is in you. Test it out. If you fail the test, do something about it. I hope the test won't show that we have failed. But if it comes to that, we'd rather the test showed our failure than yours. We're rooting for the truth to win out in you. We couldn't possibly do otherwise. We don't just put up with our limitations; we celebrate them, and then go on to celebrate every strength, every triumph of the truth in you. We pray hard that it will all come together in your lives" (2 Cor. 13:5-9, MSG).

There are events in our lives that cause us to take a good look at ourselves. The death of a close friend or loved one tends to make us stop this whirlwind of activities we call life and look deep inside our souls. Examining yourself is what the Bible teaches us to do every time we recall Jesus's death by participating in the Lord's Supper. But how do we examine ourselves? A sermon I read years ago allows me to suggest three areas that should be included as a part of our self-examination.

### Examine your relationship with God.

- Of what does our relationship with God consist? It consists of a true and total surrender of our will to the sovereign will of God, exchanging our agenda for His agenda.

- Just how committed is God to you? Well, Jesus died for you to be saved; not only for you to receive the benefits of His death, but to have complete rule over you (Rom. 14:9).

- Examine your relationship with God. Are you making your own decisions without regard to whether it is God's will or your will? Let your relationship with God be one where He rules.

### Examine your relationship with others.

- Before a person comes to God, he or she lives for him or herself because human's basic nature is self-centered. An unsaved person has little or no awareness of God's laws and has no regard for them. But when that person is saved, he or she is also transformed by the power of God. That self-centeredness is replaced with a humility and love for others. In fact, the Bible teaches what the basis of our relationship with others should be (Phil. 2:3; Rom. 12:10).

- We live in a society where we are taught to demand our rights. Christians have also demanded their right to make decisions without worrying about whether others are affected or not. They say, "I can do whatever I want. I have no obligation to other believers." The truth is No, we don't have that right, and Yes, we do have that obligation. In fact, if our actions confuse young Christians and cause them to stumble, we will be accountable to God (Matt. 18:6).

- God is committed to building a loving family, so much so that He does not even want us to approach Him if we are in conflict with a fellow believer (Matt. 5:23-24). So examine your relationship with others. Are you placing your interests and desires before others? Are you making your decisions without any consideration for how others are affected? Is there unresolved conflict with others?

Examine your relationship with the Church.

- What is this thing we call the Church? The Church is the family of God, those who are saved and transformed, and those who are called out of the world, living in community with one another. The Church meets for worship; the Church is accountable to one another; and the Church reaches out to the unsaved.

- Why is it important to be committed to the Church? Because God is committed to it, so much so that His son gave His life for the Church (Eph. 5:25). Because in being committed to it, we have power that hell itself cannot overcome (Matt. 16:18).

- Examine your relationship to the Church. Are you as committed to it as Jesus is? Are you involved in the life of the Church? Are you and your family reaping the benefits that come from being committed to the Church of God?

When we are out of line with Christian standards, we have to ask ourselves, "Am I a true Christian or am I a counterfeit?" "Am I born again or am I putting up a front?" Those of us who are Christians ought to ask ourselves that occasionally. It is a good idea to examine yourself if wrong behavior is involved.

Accountability

"Therefore encourage (admonish, exhort) one another and edify (strengthen and build up) one another, just as you are doing" (1 Thess. 5:11, AMP).

Bible.org states that by accountability, we are not talking about coercive tactics, the invasion of privacy, or bringing others under the weight of someone's taboos, legalism, or manipulative or dominating tactics. Rather, by accountability we mean developing relationships with other Christians that help to promote spiritual reality, honesty, obedience to God, and genuine evaluations of one's walk and relationship with God and with others. We are talking about relationships that help believers change by the Spirit of God and the truth of the Word of God through inward spiritual conviction and faith.

In his book, The Disciple Making Pastor, Bill Hull writes about the need for accountability in the disciple-making process. He says, "To believe you can make disciples or develop true maturity in others without accountability is like believing that you can raise children without discipline, run a company without rules, or lead an army without authority. Accountability is to the Great Commission what tracks are to a train" (152). I am convinced if you want to advance your life spiritually, personally, or professionally, you must hold yourself accountable for your actions, responsibilities, and goals. Think about it. Why should it be someone else's job to make sure you are doing the things that you know you should to be doing?

**Be accountable in your actions and choices.** This would include such things as:

- The way in which you communicate with others,
- How you spend your time,
- Your behavior and manners,
- The consideration and respect you show others,
- Your eating habits and exercise routine,
- Your attitude and thoughts, and
- The way you respond to challenges.

**Be accountable with your responsibilities.** This would include these types of things:

- Returning calls, emails, and texts promptly;
- Being on time for business and personal appointments;
- Keeping your home, car, and workplace clean;

- Spending less than you earn;
- Doing the things you agreed to do when you agreed to do them;
- Executing your job description to the best of your ability;
- Writing things down on a "To Do" list so you don't forget.

**Be accountable setting your goals**. This would include your:

- Spirituality,
- Fitness and health targets,
- Financial goals,
- Family objectives,
- Career ambitions,
- Personal goals, and
- Any other goals you have set for yourself.

Make no mistake about it. You cannot achieve any worthwhile spiritual, personal, or professional goal if you do not hold yourself accountable. The reason is simple. It is your life! Holding yourself accountable is nothing more than following through with YOUR commitments and responsibilities. It is doing what YOU know YOU should do, when YOU should it. This is your life! Take control. Be responsible for it.

## <u>L</u>ive

"After looking at the way things are on this earth, here's what I've decided is the best way to live: Take care of yourself, have a good time, and make the most of whatever job you have for as long as God gives you life. And that's about it. That's the human lot. Yes, we should make the most of what God gives, both the bounty and the capacity to enjoy it, accepting what's given and delighting in the work. It's God's gift! God deals out joy in the present, the now. It's useless to brood over how long we might live" (Eccles. 5:18-20, MSG).

When people discover the richness of life that God has provided, they do not think of the past or even talk about it. They do not talk about the future, either, because they are so involved with the savor of life right now. Many people equate being single with putting your life on hold—you are waiting to get married, waiting to have children (if you don't have any yet), waiting for the father or mother of your children to marry you—waiting. Does being single mean you have to put your life on hold? Postponing life until marriage is one of the most common traps into which singles can fall. We think, "When I'm married I'll do this . . ." or, "After I get married then I'll be happy." Because your life gets bigger every time you trust God, you have to take it one step at a time. Personally, I refused to postpone my life. I have purchased two houses, started two businesses, traveled, acquired two masters' degrees, and am now working on my doctorate degree. Speaking of traveling, since my early twenties, every year I visit a new city and every three years I travel to another country. I have not been afraid to use my talent to serve God as well. As an accomplished trainer, I travel around the United States helping pastors and church leaders with strategic planning, leadership development training, and developing healthy ministries. I serve on boards and committees that make my community a better place to live. I did not jump into all these activities at once. As I succeeded at one thing, I stepped out with another. Today, I live to make a difference because I refused to postpone my life.

Opportunities come to those who are ready for them. Though we have things we would like to do, we should always seek God for His timing. I have always wanted to get my doctorate degree, but the door did not open until I was in my forties. Ask the Lord what He will have you doing this season. I promise you, He will respond. And when He gives you the go-ahead, there will be obstacles, but . . . Don't wait.

1. *Don't wait until the situation is perfect.* You should not wait until the situation is perfect because the situation will never be perfect. No matter how or when you see it, there will always be something that make you think again.
2. *Don't wait until other people agree with you.* Just as you shouldn't wait for the situation to be perfect, you shouldn't wait until everybody agrees with your idea. There will always be opposition, and that is normal. If you wait until there is a consensus, you will never start.
3. *Don't wait until your skill is good.* We might think that we need to have a certain skill set before we start doing something. But the truth is, you will learn much more by doing than by waiting. Doing allows you to hone your skill much faster than just learning the theory.

Singles do not get hung up on wanting to be married. A young man, between the ages of 31 and 40 wrote these words: "*What God intends is for each of us to develop a walk with Him before we commit to a relationship with someone else."* Adam had a walk with God before he had a relationship with Eve. Sometimes a person, when new in the LORD at Church, will get their priorities wrong and their focus will be on finding a mate rather than building up their most Holy faith, and developing their ministry in service to the Kingdom of God. They rush into a marriage unequally yoked with unstable folks who are not mature in the LORD. The Bible teaches young men they should build their career skills and have a way to give to a family before they marry. Many rush into marriage with no skills to offer and hope the economy will always have a job; they can just get by. The marriage relationship suffers because of financial stress and then divorce. God hates divorce.

Marriage is a lifelong commitment and is not to be entered into without preparation of both the male and the female. God brings the couple together when He sees the maturity level there. Our flesh, the world, and the devil try to rush the relationship and get our priorities out of order; and the devil takes advantage of the relationship because the devil loves divorce. I have met missionaries who never have married—not because they did not want to, and not because God wanted them to be single. One missionary man was engaged to be married many years ago but rebels killed his fiancée. He never loved anyone else but her. Another single female missionary loved her home nation of Korea and such a burden to carry the Gospel to her that she just had so busy serving God in Korea she never married. Reverend Lee Stoneking is a powerful missionary evangelist to many nations. He is nearly 75 years old and has never married. He never found his equal in the LORD and did not want to put his service to God at risk with a half-hearted woman. The Bible says we are not to be unequally yoked with unbelievers, and half-hearted believers are also unbelievers.

"God created me—and you—to live with a single, all-embracing, all-transforming passion—namely, a passion to glorify God by enjoying and displaying His supreme excellence in all the spheres of life."

—John Piper, *Don't Waste Your Life*

## Life Reflections

Pray that:

- God will reveal His plan for your life

- God will heal you from past hurts and offenses

- God will give you wisdom on what to accomplish in this season of life

Consider:

1. What are you short- and long-term goals?

2. Journal how you will apply REAL to your life.

# CHAPTER 8

# Better Expectations

Feeling the pressure to live up to everyone else's expectations is something to be reckoned with by all. Singles tend to place their expectations in others and make decisions based how others expect us to be. From those we respect and trust, expectations can have a powerful impact. Rising to meet the expectations of others can lead to either improvement or destruction. Whether you realize it or not, we all accept expectations from those in our circle. At church, we see others standing, then we stand. If one person claps, others will clap. When you were younger, if somebody in crowd started running, afterward the entire crowd ran. Those we believe in and hang around stimulate us. On the other hand, we develop expectations for other people. We expect others to treat us a certain way and do what we want. When you go to work, you expect to get a paycheck. Sometimes we will not even make our expectations known. But when our expectations are not met, we are upset because we were looking forward to something without making our anticipation known. We use this same attitude toward our relationship with God. We fall out with Him when our expectations in life are not met.

Most times, the expectation for God to work in our life is based on another person conforming to what we want. But He wants us to set our expectations on and in Him. This is one of the greatest developments you can have as a Christian single. God is the one who will not fail you in life. He is waiting to fulfill your expectations that line up with His will for you. He will not and cannot work outside of the principles in the Word of God. Isaiah said it best, " And therefore the Lord [earnestly] waits [expecting, looking, and longing] to be gracious to you;

and therefore He lifts Himself up, that He may have mercy on you and show loving-kindness to you. For the Lord is a God of justice. Blessed (happy, fortunate, to be envied) are all those who [earnestly] wait for Him, who expect and look and long for Him [for His victory, His favor, His love, His peace, His joy, and His matchless, unbroken companionship]!" (Isa. 30:18, AMP). Expectation is something looked forward to not hoped for or feared.

Imagine a college student going to class, and week after week completing assignments and taking tests. They do the work expecting that one day they will earn enough credits to obtain a degree. If they are convinced they could not pass, do you think they would engage in the course work? Absolutely not, it would be a waste of time. But if they believed that in the end they would acquire a degree, they would go to class with an expectation. They complete the work with the understanding that is necessary to reap the harvest (the degree). The following passage brings this same illustration to life. "Of course. Farmers plow and thresh expecting something when the crop comes in. So if we have planted spiritual seed among you, is it out of line to expect a meal or two from you? Others demand plenty from you in these ways. Don't we who have never demanded deserve even more?" (1 Cor. 9:10-12, MSG). Between believing and manifestation, most people make plans for fulfillment without ever expressing their expectations. When you are expecting, you put all your effort into expecting your needs to be supplied. I have found this to be false with most Christians. We spend most of our time finding ways around the issue instead of having an attitude of expectation. Then, when our expectations are not met, we are affected—always expecting the worst. I am not in the world to live up to your expectations, neither are you here to live up to mine. We are called to lower our expectation in people and increase our expectation in God. Without God, people succeed in bringing out the worse in one another. We tend to deal with one another unfairly or try to be all things to all people.

> Between *believing* and *manifestation,* most people make plans for **fulfillment** without ever expressing their **expectation**

Sometimes we can have false expectations. I have met people exhausted with waiting for God to move. I have tasted that exhaustion myself, as a ministry worker for over 15 years. God was moving, but because of how I expected Him to move, I could not see it. Sometimes when God worked, it did not feel like a move of the Spirit. Sometimes when God spoke, I locked myself into an imagination of how I thought it should happen. When God showed up a different way, sometimes I got it and sometimes I did not. In 2000, Stan Smith wrote an article called "Crippled by False Expectations" (www.elijahlist.com). First, he discussed the Naaman Principle from 2 Kings 5. The noted miracle almost aborted because of false expectations. Naaman was a military man who also was a leper. When he visited the prophet Elisha, Elisha's servant told Naaman to go wash in the Jordan seven times. Well, Naaman was expecting to see the prophet himself. Because his expectations were not met, he became angry at God's methods. After complaining awhile, he obeyed. Smith highlights that "faith and expectation work together— Naaman expected to be healed." He almost missed his miracle because of his expectation of how God would do it. Naaman's expectation was good, but he could not put God in a box. If your expectation helps you find God, then go with it. If it is frustrating, then release it. What is your story?

Female, Age Range: 31-40

*For years, I lived and tried to succeed off what others expected of me. Then, I decided to live by what I expected. Let me tell you, neither way worked for me. That was a complete setup for FAILURE, and when I crashed, I crashed HARD. I've learned a very important lesson within these past three years of my life. I learned that what others outside of God expected of me never mattered. I also learned that my way (my expectations) were harming me both mentally and physically. But the greatest lesson learned was, if I surrendered to God and allowed Him to take the lead, I could bear witness to His wonders.*

*Daily, I surrender and expect God to take the lead. I no longer place unrealistic expectations upon myself. Instead, I ask Him, "What is it you wish (expect) me to do today, Father?" When I quiet my chaotic mind and meet with Him in prayer, He shows me His expectations for that day. He never shows me weeks, months, or years down the line. He is very realistic! He gets that we humans can handle things day by day, and so that is how He operates with me. He frees me from stress, anger, hurt, and disappointment by doing this. I expect to be joyful, glad, happy, kind, compassionate, successful, and blessed. I expect all of these things not by what man says, but by what His Words tell me. I know through Him, through surrendering each day in total Faith, I WILL be granted these things. I place my expectations in the palm of His hands and He blesses me. I expect nothing more than what He has to offer me, and THAT is all I need in this life.*

Two principles that will help you keep your expectation in the right perspective:

1. Hold Fast (Heb. 10:23). Two things you will learn from this passage; wavering is possible and God is faithful. It is easy to waver, and protection from it is not automatic. The word confession implies, "to say a like word" or "to say the same as the Word says agreeing with the word of God." We should let our expectation show by our speech and our actions; our talk and our walk. Everything you do should show that your expectation is in God. My expectation in God is that others will deal with me with pure motives. If this is not the case, then it's not God. So then, I have to make a decision to separate. Bottom line: what you are expecting will come out of your conversation. It is when you are not convinced that you waver. In the 1860s, C. Blodin pushed a wheelbarrow across the Niagara Falls on a tight rope. The crowd cheered at his accomplishment. But when invited, none of the crowd was willing to get in the barrow—although they all were living witnesses. The spectators wavered because they weren't 100% convinced that he could do it with a rider. As it relates to expectation, they believed—but no action followed. Holding fast to your confession will always lead to action. All you have in this life is believing and renewing your mind so that your confession agrees with the Word. Expressing your faith without words is dead faith!

2. Be Thankful in Faith for the Results (Col. 2:7). Thanksgiving is a public celebration in acknowledgement of divine favor, an expression of gratitude and grateful feelings or thoughts. Work on the habit of thanking God for results in your life. The more you give thanks and show gratitude to God, the more your expectation becomes rooted in Him and not others. Thanking God keeps Him in your expectations until they become reality. When you take Him out, you take matters into your own hand; or you begin to pull the strings and create your own picture. The story is told of a young woman believing God for a job. She started very strong believing God; she prayed and thanked Him daily. Months went by and she was still unemployed. Growing weary, she kept praying but stopped thanking Him in her prayers. This young woman stopped lifting up her situation in prayer and started doing things her way. She embellished her resume, putting her expectations in others and relied on her physical attributes to get

a job. Of course, she got a position—but it did not last. Tired of waiting on God, she stepped out of character.

I hear countless stories like this when it comes to singles desiring a mate (male and female). There was a season in my life that I got tired of waiting. For a short span of time, I took matters into my hands. But when the Holy Spirit showed me the outcome, I redirected my expectation back to God. Like me, when you veer away from the prompting of the Holy Spirit you will experience brokenness. When I stopped praying about my desires and thanking God for results, my faith weakened for the manifestation. I lowered my standards and my priority became what I wanted and not what God wanted for me. I realized that when my focus changed, the motive of my desires changed. When your desires change, you can lose hope. And when you lose hope, you run the risk of considering or doing ungodly things to achieve your desired outcome. I had not gone on a date in years, forgetting what it felt like to be in the presence of a man. Although I knew our spiritual perspectives were different, I allowed myself to be lured in by the attention a particular person was giving. Playing with fire, I continued to spend time with him knowing the risk and price was higher than I was willing to consume. Though I liked him and the attention he gave, I had to walk away. This is why it's important to thank God for who He is, what He does, and what He gives.

Such thankfulness keeps our expectations in and on Him. You cannot overdo it when giving thanks. Abounding in it with thanksgiving is over and beyond in measure or number. I am convinced that Satan can trick us out of our abundant life. You start strong, operating in the principle; if the answer takes longer than you anticipated, you drop the expectation. God says, "Patient endurance is what you need now, so that you will continue to do God's will. Then you will receive all that He has promised" (Heb. 10:36, NLT). As we consider the parable about the mustard seed, notice it became a large tree. When you plant seeds, do you expect a harvest? Every May, I buy plants for my flowerbeds. When I plant them, I expect them to grow and multiply. If my expectations are not met, then I am disappointed. But I can't plant them and then never give them water or care; they would wither away. Many times, we have unexpressed and cultivated expectations. Before an expectation can be met, you have to first plant the seed. I also like the story in Acts 3: the man who lay at the gate called beautiful expected to receive something from Peter and John. He got more than he was looking for.

*Will you dare to risk expecting great things from God in and through your life this year that will bring Him glory! It's so easy to retreat into a mindset of what we can't do. Great expectations come from putting your faith in what God can do. The great missionary William Carey put it like this: "Expect great things from God. Attempt great things for God." Faith is expecting God to come through and do great things in your life. Pray that God will break through the mental barriers in your life that have prevented you from expecting great things.*

Someone shared with me seven ways to increase my level of expectation and now I'm sharing them with you:

1. Believe that God has placed the seeds of a great harvest within you and acknowledge those seeds.

2. Plant your seeds.

3. Plant many seeds. To paraphrase the words of Paul, "Sow a lot, reap a lot" (2 Cor. 9:6). In those seasons of my life when I was applying for jobs, I learned that my chances of employment increased as the number of applications I submitted to different employers increased.

4. Plant seeds even when it is difficult. Solomon said, "He who observes the wind will not sow, and he who observes the clouds will not reap" (Eccles. 11:4). The Psalmist said, "Those who sow in tears shall reap in joy" (Ps. 126:5). We are not promised picture-perfect scenarios wherein we can plant our seeds. We have to live by a "sow anyway" mentality.

5. Don't give up. Paul said, "And let us not grow weary while doing good, for in due season we shall reap if we do not lose heart" (Gal. 6:9). Just because you do not see results to-

day doesn't mean there will not be results.

6. Work your field with hope. Even if you don't see anything, things are at work. All the work you are doing, planting and working your field, will pay off. Maybe not today or tomorrow, but there will be a day when all your "plowing efforts" kick in! Paul tells us, "He who plows should plow in hope" (1 Cor. 9:10). Solomon reminds everyone there is "much food in the fallow ground of the poor" (Prov. 13:23). No matter who we are or what situation we find ourselves in, "much" is connected to our "seed."

7. Our expectation level should be raised because God is the "Lord of the harvest" (Matt. 9:38). No one else is in charge of our harvest. It doesn't matter what situation, predicament, or problem we face. We should believe in the power and potential of the seed that God has given us. May we never forget that God can make the "desert" of our life "like the garden of the Lord" (Isa. 51:3).

One of my favorite blog spots is Kerry Shook Ministries. This year, he posted the following about expectations:

*What are you expecting in 2014? Most of us begin with making plans and then setting goals to carry out those plans. It's conventional wisdom. But this year I want to challenge you to think. Instead of starting with your plans of what you want to achieve, begin with your expectations. What are you expecting God to do in and through your life this year? This is what I call "the faith factor." It causes us to look beyond what we can do, or more often, what we think we can't do, and focus on what God can do. Then when God comes through, even your critics will have to give God the credit. Everyone will know it must have been God! Think of the glory and honor He would receive if the only explanation for what is happening in your life was God. The truth is we get out of life about what we expect. Jesus said we get to decide what we want God to do in our lives in this regard. In Matthew 9, Jesus encounters two blind men who are calling out to Him, "Son of David, have mercy on us!" Jesus asked them, "Do you believe that I am able to do this?" They replied, "Yes, Lord." Then Matthew tells us that Jesus touched their eyes and said, "According to your faith will it be done to you."*

*So what about it? Will you dare to risk expecting great things from God in and through your life this year that will bring Him glory! It's so easy to retreat into a mindset of what we can't do. Great expectations come from putting your faith in what God can do. The great missionary William Carey put it like this: "Expect great things from God. Attempt great things for God." Faith is expecting God to come through and do great things in your life. Pray that God will break through the mental barriers in your life that have prevented you from expecting great things. Keep those expectations before God in prayer and let Him show Himself mighty in your life! Ephesians 3:20 is my prayer for you. "Now all glory to God, who is able, through His mighty power at work within us, to accomplish infinitely more than we might ask or think."*

"Instead of imagining all the things we can accomplish, we ask God to do what only He can accomplish. Yes, we work, we plan, we organize, and we create, but we do it all while we fast, while we pray, and while we constantly confess our need for the provision of God."

—David Platt, *Radical: Taking Back Your Faith from the American Dream*

## Life Reflections

Pray that:

- God will give you vision this season of your life

- God will renew your mind

- God will show you how to put your expectation in Him

Consider:

1. What are your expectations for the next 12 months?

2. What goals are associated with your expectations?

# CHAPTER 9

# Breathtaking Grace

Grace Great (name changed) got married at age 18. She divorced after 16 years because of her husband's infidelity and drug addiction. He was her childhood sweetheart and the only man she knew. After the divorce, she relocated to be closer to her family. Grace searched and searched but could not find a church home that reminded her of the church she left. Divorced, lonely, and raising three kids on her own provoked curiosity. She began to examine her sisters' lives; they were dating, going out, and seemed happy. She decided to get on board. Such thoughts lead her into a three-year fornication spiral. She then found a church home and tried to live a righteous life, but after six months found herself in the bed with yet another man, continuing in the spirit of fornication. Grace got tired and decided to repent and confess to her current pastor. She was advised not to worry about it—everybody has shortcomings. In her heart, she wanted correction and rebuking; in her mind that pastor failed her. She eventually landed where she felt she could blossom and grow. She began to study the Word, get active in church, and connect. Many things led to her deliverance. However, she shared one incident in particular: One day during the act of sex with her love interest, God flashed her pastor's face before her eyes. She realized in an instant that God was watching her, and that she needed to repent to God and not man. After that night, Grace cold turkey quit fornicating. Upon repenting, she did not struggle with receiving God's GRACE. There was no condemnation, and she took a stand for righteousness. Even though she had stopped fornicating, she still needed deliverance from the soul ties that kept popping up like pennies. Per Grace, soul ties are the reason many of us cannot receive His GRACE.

A soul tie is not a word you will find in the Bible. The word describes relationships established with others. It is considered a knitting together of two souls (spiritually) that can bring either great blessings or grave destruction. It can also be described as "cleave," which means to bring close together, to follow close after, to be attached to someone, or to adhere to one another as with glue. As soul tie in a marriage relationship is good; in an unmarried relationship, destructive and ungodly. Ungodly soul ties leave you fragmented and unable to be joined to anybody. They are formed by close relationships, like David and Jonathan's, whose relationship was good. But such ties can also be formed from toxic relationships. Bad soul ties will cause you to stay in relationships of abuse, provoking you to run *to* them—instead of running *away*. Such soul ties are born from communicating and spending time with someone whose conduct does not line up with the Word of God. They are created by allowing him or her to whisper sweet nothings in your ear, touch you in intimate places, kiss you, and manipulate you. As you can see, the soul tie does not just result from sex. Conversation, spending time together, and so on are strong links to wrong soul ties. The stronger the bonding or soul tie between two people, the deeper and more lasting the relationship. The emotional and mental strengths of one sustain the other in times of adversity. Good soul ties allow two people to rejoice with each other in times of difficulty and triumph.

Soul ties can also be used for the devil's advantage. Ties formed from sex outside of marriage cause a person to become defiled. "And when Shechem the son of Hamor the Hivite, prince of the country, saw her, he took her, and lay with her, and defiled her. And his soul clave unto Dinah the daughter of Jacob, and he loved the damsel, and spake kindly unto the damsel" (Gen. 34:2-3, KJV). Why is it common for a person to still have "feelings" toward an ex-lover that they have no right to be attracted to in that way? Even 20 years down the road, a person may still think of their first lover . . . even if he or she is across the country and has their own family—all because of a soul tie! Soul ties are usually between two people, but you can become tied to a family, friends, co-workers, leadership, customer, client, and so forth. The oneness or unity that we share with others is an expression of our soul ties. When you allow ungodly soul ties, you are one soul tied to many partners. Take the sexual soul tie, for example. If you have sex with a prostitute, you have become one with her or him. If you are married and commit adultery, you are now tied to your wife and your lover. If you allow a soul tie with a friend who does not have your same value system, you become knitted to them.

When a woman becomes pregnant, she carries the baby inside of her for nine months; during that time, she and the baby are one. The umbilical cord connects the mother to the baby. The baby receives all the nutrients from the mother. They have to go everywhere together. When the mother experiences stress, anger, bitterness, and other things, the baby is affected. Once the baby is born, the mother and the baby are still connected by the umbilical cord, and a procedure has to be done to separate the two—the umbilical cord has to be cut. When this happens, the baby can begin its new life. This is a great example of what God is trying to show us about being soul tied. You have to cut and sever all old ties before you start your new life. You can see the importance of severing the spiritual umbilical cord from those in the past. As long as you are connected in the soul of someone from the past, you will struggle to move forward to your future.

*The oneness or unity that we share with others is an expression of our soul ties.*

So many single people want to get married but are not ready. They have to prepare themselves for their new bride or groom. The most important thing is to get rid of the old to allow the new to come forth. If you go into a marriage with all your past life ties severed, the enemy will try to bring them back. Let's say you are married and your spouse starts cheating on you. He or she comes home late from work; you receive hang-up calls; you became suspicious of your spouse's every move. You divorce and later meet someone else and decide to marry. One night, your new spouse is late coming home, and the phone rings—then a hang up. The devil starts putting thoughts in your mind that your new spouse is cheat-ing on you, just as the other did; the devil goes on and on. By the time your spouse walks in the house, you are in a rage. You start accusing them of all the things your ex- spouse did to you. Can you see what is happening here? You are repeating your past, because you have not released the other person from your soul. If not dealt with, it becomes a never-ending cycle. You can try to deal with it in the natural by seeing counselors, trying to forget, or by even getting a di-vorce—but those are temporary. It must be dealt with in the spiritual realm. Terri Savelle of Foy Ministries (www.terri.com) taught about four indicators of wrong soul ties.

1. **"I feel so confused."** When you are outside the will of God in a particular relationship, you will experience confusion. Your feelings will tell you one thing; your spirit will tell you another. That's where the confusion comes in. "God is not the author of confusion but of peace" (1 Cor. 14:33, KJV). If you are not experiencing peace in this relationship, or "soul tie," then something is not right. That is the Holy Spirit warning you and working to get your attention. You need to respect these warnings. They are not to be brushed off or treated as a small thing. Honor the Holy Spirit's leading in your life. You should not feel confused if you are in the will of God. Honestly, why would you want to be any other place? When you are confused about a relationship, you can make unwise, regretful decisions. You need to take purposeful steps to feed your spirit the truth of God's Word. The truth always overrides deception.

2. **"I'm just miserable."** When we persist in doing something that we know God is not in agreement with, we will experience misery that doesn't go away. You may feel uneasy inside or extreme anxiety, sorrow, or pain. You may feel disgusted by what you're doing, yet powerless to change your situation. Those are all indicators that Satan is at work in your life to destroy it. David cried out in Ps. 38:8, "I am exhausted and completely crushed. My groans come from an anguished heart" (NLT). If that describes how you feel when you're alone, Ps. 23:3 says, "He restores my soul" (NIV). Those four little words will redefine your life. God will restore your mind, your will, and your emotions.

3. **"My mind is tormented."** The mind of Christ is one that is at peace no matter what the circumstances. When Satan has invaded our souls through wrong soul ties, our minds will not be at rest. This is where your battle takes place. Is your mind replaying images of the past and rehearsing earlier conversations like a broken record? Do your thoughts produce fear or make you feel unclean? Whatever is going on in your mind is affecting your emotional state. Your feelings are indicators of what you are thinking. 2 Cor. 10:5 says that we are to renew our minds by taking "captive every thought to make it obedient to Christ" (NIV). I will be the first to admit that it's not easy, but it is necessary. You can do this. As a Christian, you can get your thoughts under the control of your reborn spirit. How? By speaking God's Word out of your mouth every single time a negative thought enters your mind. Don't just think it, speak it. It can be

as simple as saying, "Thank You, Lord, that You restore my soul" over and over and over. Be persistent. Satan hates nothing more than to hear you speak the Word of God and the name of Jesus!

4. **"I didn't mean to disobey God . . . on purpose."** If you feel like you have been dealing with a situation far too long and nothing seems to help you get beyond it, remember this phrase: God will not advance your instructions beyond your last act of disobedience. If you don't obey what God is telling you to do, you will never move beyond your current circumstances. I don't know what that means to you, but I know what it meant for me years ago. I was desperate to move beyond my circumstances, no matter how painful it would be.

"God's grace is upon you and me for forgiveness and overcoming soul ties."

When a person who is bonded to another is governed by impure motives or the want for selfish gain, the soul tie between them can enable (make able) that selfishness to manipulate and abuse the other. A person can control another through soul ties because the minds of the two are open to one another. In ungodly relationships, these ties may place you in emotional and mental bondage to others. In turn, you will find yourself saying things to your own hurt. Bad soul ties can happen between two Christians if they are engaging in works of the flesh. Because both profess Christianity does not mean that God is in the relationship. I once allowed an ungodly soul tie with a Christian of the opposite sex. Realizing I had relaxed my own standard by not keeping Christ at the center of the association. The soul tie formed through communication, spending time together, and sharing intimate details about my life. I made bad decisions, but spiritual matters were still my priority. This soul tie impacted me the same as a sexual soul tie. Although I was enjoying the attention, I drew strength from my desire to do things God's way—to walk away. That's not to say that I will not mess up again, but true repentance changed the "want to" in me. God's grace is upon you and me for forgiveness and overcoming soul ties. What you need is more grace! Maybe you have regrets and are now doing your best to live for God. Do not lose hope. God's grace is enough to cover your sin and help you move on. However, others are still wavering. Obedience to God looks boring; pursuing the world and its pleasure appears tantalizing. Please take to heart this warning from this chapter. May it shock you and sober you—and in doing so, lead you to life.

A *Word Book* article written by N. H. Snaith states there is a distinction between the use of the word "grace" in the Old and New Testaments. In the Old Testament, it can be used to describe kindness and graciousness in general, with no particular tie or personal relationship between the individuals involved, or as shown by a superior to an inferior when there is no obligation to do so. Its use in the Old Testament also signifies a specific kindness that gives pleasure to both giver and receiver, thereby implying a special relationship between them. On the other hand, in the New Testament, "grace" indicates God's redemptive love is always active to save the people and to keep them in relationship with God. In this way, it implies God's continual, unfailing faithfulness both to His covenant and to His people forever.

Yet how do we understand, how do we experience, grace today? I often think of it in terms of a statement I once heard: "You are accepted." You and I are accepted, fully and totally accepted, by God—now, always, without condition, without deserving, without question. To be accepted in this way means to be cherished, to be loved, to be guarded, from ultimate evil. It means that who we are is valued, honored, and respected. It means that we do not have to earn or deserve such care; it is there for us, ours as an outright gift. The grace of God is given to us at God's initiative. It expresses God's love for us, God's desire, God's unconditional acceptance; it expresses the very nature of God's being. It does not matter how long you have been walking with Christ, or the offenses you committed, the same amount of grace is available for all.

The author Frederick Buechner, in his book Wishful Thinking, puts it this way: "The grace of God means something like: Here is your life. You might never have been, but you are because the party would not have been complete without you. Here is the world. Beautiful and terrible things will happen. Do not be afraid. I am with you. Nothing can ever separate us. It is for you I created the universe. I love you but there is one catch. Like any other gift, the gift of grace can be yours if you will reach out and take it. Maybe being able to reach out and take it is a gift too."

Grace is mercy, clemency, and pardon. Biblically, grace is unmerited favor. It is God's free action for the help of His people. It is different from justice and mercy. Justice is getting what we deserve. Mercy is not getting what we deserve. Grace is getting what we do not deserve. Consider these three aspects of grace: saving grace, sustaining grace, and sanctifying grace.

- Saving Grace - In 2 Timothy 1:9, Paul speaks of God who has saved us—not because of our works but because of His own purpose and grace. This grace is given to us by Christ Jesus. God's greatest demonstration of grace is seen in Jesus Christ! WITHOUT JESUS, THERE IS NO GRACE! Jesus is the very personification of God's grace! And His death on the cross was the "greatest show on earth" of God's grace!

- Sustaining Grace - Romans 4:7-8 says you are blessed because your sins are covered and they won't count against you. Why is it that the Lord will never count our sins against us at death or at the judgment? IT'S BECAUSE OF JESUS! And it's because we've put our trust and our hope in Him and Him alone! Our sins are covered by His blood! He bore our sins in His body on the tree! He became sin for us so that in Him we might become the righteousness of God! God's grace sustains us in this way and we need to learn to walk with our heads held high! And there should be some spring in our walk and our talk! We should live a joyous life because we know where we're headed. AND IT'S ALL BECAUSE OF JESUS!

- Sanctifying Grace - Titus 2:11-12 teaches that God's grace appeared to all, giving us the power to say no to sin and live a life of self-control. The grace of God should sanctify us. Sanctification is the act of becoming holy, and this process should start when we come in contact with God's grace and surrender our lives to Jesus Christ. The grace of God should motivate us to live right. It should be a controlling power in our lives. Brethren, we admit that we all sin. Don't ever be so proud as to say you don't sin. WE ALL SIN AND WE ALL STRUGGLE WITH SIN DAILY (Rom. 3:23). But the grace of God is supposed to change us into better people.

*"God's grace sus-tains us in this way and we need to learn to walk with our heads held high!"*

Sustaining and sanctifying grace are where I believe most struggle. To live in His grace, we must understand and believe that He is a forgiving God, and He desires for us to live the abundant life. God is patient with us and willing to work through the process with us. You have messed up. Well, so have I. Not to mention there were many others in the Bible who messed up. David, a man after God's own heart, wrote the 51st Division Psalms as a result of his mess up. Peter messed up several times, to include denying Jesus. Paul said in Romans 7 that he does not practice what he should, because of the sin that dwells in him. And consider that Paul was like our modern-day bishop when he wrote that. Read what this woman of God had to say:

...YOU EXPERIENCE **GRACE** WHEN YOU CAN LOOK PAST YOUR IMPERFECTIONS TO SEE THE PERSON GOD CREATED AND NOT HOLD YOURSELF HOSTAGE TO THE ACTIONS YOU COMMITTED.

> *My husband says sin happens in increments and shame slowly creeps in, robbing you of joy. I found myself active in my church, with young women looking to me as a role model, and yet my past sins haunted me through embarrassing and painful memories. As I grew in my faith, I became more and more disappointed that I had not been stronger in those early years. My healing process started through sharing with women friends, praying, and praying some more. I felt God's forgiveness as counseling, reading, studying Scripture, and healing prayer became significant stages of that process. But it wasn't easy. It was long, twisted, and painful. One experience was particularly helpful. At one prayer meeting, some women were praying for me. My feet felt heavy, as if encased in cement. I described the sensation and began sharing my past sin experiences. As I received their love and assurances of forgiveness, the cement broke into pieces, and soon I felt as if my feet were in dancing shoes! I felt free of the shame and bondage of my past, and I felt God's love and forgiveness deep within my bones. That prayer meeting was just one of many steps in the healing process for me.*

Grace is the face love when it meets imperfection. Jesus was sentenced for all the sins we have committed and for those yet to come. You experience grace when you can look past your imperfections to see the person God created and not hold yourself hostage to the actions you committed. It is also looking past the actions of others, not beating them over the head with them. God freely gives each one of us grace. Grace is always on the giving end and we are on the receiving end. This is so beyond our grasp that I really don't think that we will understand it until we meet God face to face.

"Come now, and let us reason together, says the Lord. Though your sins are like scarlet, they shall be as white as snow; though they are red like crimson, they shall be like wool." (Isa. 1:18)

Jill Briscoe once wrote that Isaiah's messages brought comfort among God's people who were true believers. Isaiah reminded them of the "covenant of grace." At the same time, he brought a message of severe warning to those who refused to listen to the doctrine of life. When the Lord called His rebellious people to "reason together," He did not call them to debate, but rather to agree with, His verdict. He wanted them to acknowledge that their actions had not been following reason.

All sin is unreasonable. The people's sin is described as scarlet—in contrast to the stark whiteness of snow—and crimson—as opposed to the whiteness of wool. Crimson yarn in biblical times meant that the yarn had gone through two baths, or double dying. When Christ forgave my sin, I was very conscious that grace invited not a dialogue but a reasonable confession of the "double-dyed" mess I had made of my life. God wanted me to agree with His verdict and submit to His decision about my sin. I felt like a small ship whose wool had been dyed crimson by wrongdoing, and I was pretty red-faced about it all.

One key to living in God's grace is remembering it is His idea. Getting caught up in your own works takes the focus off God. Perfection is not a prerequisite to receiving God's grace. Max Lucado said, "To discover grace is to discover God's utter devotion to you, His stubborn resolve to give you a cleansing, healing, purging love that lifts the wounded back to their feet." Another key is forgiveness. Oftentimes, we ask for forgiveness but still have a hard time believing that God forgave us. Take a few moments to worship and praise God. Sing or dance, but express yourself with purity in heart. As His goodness becomes more meaningful in your heart, receiving His grace becomes easier. Loving others is paramount to grasping the heart of God. Lastly, give away grace. My challenge for you is to practice giving grace to someone, so you can learn to receive grace. I had the pleasure of seeing the movie The Grace Card. In this movie, a young African American Pastor (Police Officer) took on the challenge of decreasing racism in his community. He came up with the concept of giving someone a "grace card" when mistreated instead of calling a person to the carpet. In the movie a young African American male accidently killed a young Caucasian boy. Toward the end of the movie, the killer came face to face with the murdered boy's father. He apologized for taking the boy's life. The father was speechless, so he reached into his pocket and pulled out a "grace card" and handed it to the man. He then embraced him with tears in his eyes. Wow, I don't think there was a dry eye in the theatre. I learned an awesome lesson from this movie about extending grace.

Anyone who knows me, knows that I am a stickler for time—because it is the only thing you cannot recapture. Several of my friends are always late. I would usually rag on them for their lateness, but I surprised one of my friends one day. I gave him a piece of paper denoted as a "grace card," with his name on it. Showing grace means letting someone off the hook for his or her action. You'll be amazed at how overwhelming that feeling can be when you just give God the glory through it all. What joy to enter the "covenant of grace" and experience the whiteness of the soul that coming to God brings! Have you come to the point of accepting God's verdict of your life, or are you still arguing your case?

---

"Grace isn't just forgiveness, it is forgiveness fueled by surrender."

—Amy E. Spiegel, *Letting Go of Perfect: Women, Expectations, and Authenticity*

**Life Reflections**

Pray for:

- Soul ties and strong holds to be destroyed over your life

- Growth in grace and love

- God's favor upon your life

Consider:

1. Are you ready to receive God's grace? Why?

2. How did this chapter impact your life?

# Beautiful Encouragement...

My sisters and brothers, the abundant life God wants you to live is more than material gain. Many singles are confused about what they should be doing while single. I give this encouragement according to John 10:10. Jesus says that He came so that you may have life more abundantly. Living abundantly may mean to you excelling in your career and having material things to prove it. Like me, you've probably heard all of your life to get your education, set up your career, buy the house or car you want, and travel. You should want to do all those things; but those accomplishments are not the sum of who you are and who God intends for you to be. Neither was Jesus referring to those things. But the void of a spouse can lead you down the road of impressing others with worldly success.

When Jesus spoke of living the abundant life, He was talking about spiritually. God's grace, mercy, acceptance, and love are the cornerstones of John 10:10. Unlike money, all these cornerstones last for eternity. Spiritual maturity breeds the wisdom to discern between what is true and what is false. Maturity helps you see through status symbols and know that God is not impressed by them. Abundant living is learning to trust God more than yourself. Trusting yourself and your abilities is what created havoc in your life to date. Abundant living is a matter of attitude and putting God above anything else. You must have appreciation for the wealth God placed in you—in peace of mind, confidence, inner joy, and love. You can have a lot of money and not be wealthy or ever find peace. Only you can get your attitude about God right. You will discover that living the abundant life is possible regardless of your marital status. Now the question becomes, will you obey God so you can live the abundant life?

There are at least three different reasons why people might obey God. First, they might be motivated by fear and don't want to face the punishment. God wants us to respect His power, but He does not want us to be motivated into following Him out this fear. Second, they may obey to receive something or get what they want. This describes someone who is "going through the motions," but their heart isn't into it because their real motivation is just their own selfish gain. Third, because of the love they have for their Father. Children who love their parents do not want to disappoint them. Which person will you be?

Most singles imagine that in God's eyes we are just one of millions. We know most people don't think we are important, and so we assume that God thinks of us in a similar way. But then again, God is not like "most people." We feel that God has favorites and we think we're a fair way down the list, but these feelings do not correspond to reality. To God, we are special.

*Alisa*

Thank you for your support. I pray this book was a blessing to you.

To order additional copies of this book, to invite Alisa to speak at your event, or to bring a workshop to your ministry, contact:

*Alisa J. Henley*

CALLED TO REBUILD LIVES!

Alisa J. Henley

PO Box 683

Grandview, MO 64030

1 888 851 5554

info@alisahenley.com

www.alisahenley.com

For ministry consulting services, visit www.u-shine.org.

Other published books:

Catch The Vision, Stay the Course!
ISBN: 978-0-9646543-5-8

www.ingramcontent.com/pod-product-compliance
Lightning Source LLC
LaVergne TN
LVHW081328060426
835513LV00012B/1223